SAVING PROGRESSIVE CHRISTIANITY TO SAVE THE PLANET

BRUCE EPPERLY

Energion Publications
Cantonment, Florida
2024

Cover Design: Henry Neufeld
Cover Image: Adobe Stock

ISBN: 978-1-63199-921-5
eISBN: 978-1-63199-922-2
Library of Congress Control Number: 2024948482

Energion Publications
1241 Conference Rd
Cantonment, FL 32533

(850) 525-3916

pubs@energion.com

TABLE OF CONTENTS

THE BIRTH OF THIS TEXT

This text was conceived on January 6, 2021, the Feast of Epiphany, the day of the Magi's visitation to the baby Jesus. I experienced an illumination that day, but not the one I expected, as I watched in horror as hordes of my fellow Americans stormed the USA Capitol, overpowering Capitol police in search of elected representatives and occupying the Halls of Congress. With murder on their minds, the lawless mob attempted to nullify the peaceful transition of power that has characterized the American political ethos from the beginning of our republic's history.

I had a deeper illumination as I observed the composition of the crowd and this involved the state of Christianity in the United States. My horror at the Capitol carnage turned to prophetic indignation as I saw videos of my Christian kin bowing in prayer and then charging toward the Capitol, filled with vengeance and prepared to mete out retribution, with many of the prayer warriors, chanting "Kill Mike Pence," Donald Trump's Vice President and a devout fundamentalist Christian, simply for following the Constitution. While not all the insurrectionists were Christian, Jesus' name was invoked as the Senate chamber was breached by the insurrectionists, many of whom saw themselves as doing God's will in overturning a fair and honest election. Signs proclaimed "Jesus is my Savior. Trump is my President," equating God's will and Trump's as one seamless reality.

Epiphany is a day of revealing and illumination, and certainly January 6, 2021, was a day in which many of our Christian kin revealed their true loyalties. Conflating loyalty to Trump with faithfulness to Christ, the insurrectionists willfully abandoned Jesus as their spiritual and moral leader and turned their backs on God's aim at Shalom. A prevaricating and power-hungry celebrity politician, known for his embrace of the seven deadly sins and fomenting of hate and incivility, eclipsed Jesus the healer, mystic, prophet, and friend of the vulnerable and stranger. Drunk on the love of power, the Christians among the insurrectionists saw themselves as God's avenging angels, crusaders against abortion and LGBTQ+ rights, the poisonous influence of immigrant vermin, the threat to marriage posed by women's rights, and the danger of diversity of religions and cultures. Climate denial and vaccine conspiracy theories as well as fear of drag queens inspired their crusade to take back America and create a fundamentalist Christian nation. In their minds, Christianity was under attack and their chosen secular savior Donald Trump was being martyred for his unapologetic support of the old-time religion of Christian nationalism, male domination, white privilege, unfettered capitalism, and racial purity.

Certain that God was on their side, the January 6 rioters were ready to mow down anyone who stood in the way of their desire to establish a truly Christian nation. They saw themselves embodying the spirit of the hymn "Onward Christian soldiers, marching as to war, with the cross of Jesus going on before." Tragically, there was no salvation or grace in the crusaders' message of violence and destruction. There was no opportunity for reconciliation or forgiveness in relationship with their opponents. Nor did the insurrectionists embody Jesus' love for his enemies and hospitality to strangers and aliens.

I was appalled that the "evangelical" Christians rioting in the Capitol and those who marched lock step with Donald Trump's agenda were perceived by the media and many persons outside Christian faith to be the primary representatives of what it means to be a Christian today. I was also discouraged by the apparent eclipse of open-spirited progressive religion as a positive force in politics and the national dialogue. "Did progressives still have a place in creatively shaping the spiritual and political future of the United States?" I pondered. "Or were our voices being drowned out by the angry crusaders of the Christian right?"

January 6 also revealed something important for my understanding of the role progressive Christians are challenged to play in the future of our nation and American Christianity. I have come to see the significance for our nation and the planet of a robust, spiritually inspired, and politically minded progressive Christianity as a spiritual alternative to and firewall mitigating the dangers of conservative Christian white nationalism and the idolatry Trump Church. No longer willing to hide our message under a bushel basket, or complacently believe that "it can't happen here," I believe progressive Christianity can be a positive force in healing our nation and the planet. While recognizing the importance of pluralism, the non-establishment of any religious tradition, and the reality that not all conservative Christians are white nationalists and aspiring insurrectionists, progressive Christians have a mission to be God's companions in healing persons, communities, nations, and our planet. We are called to follow in the footsteps of the Hebraic prophets, the ministry of Jesus, the early Christian movement, abolitionists, the German confessing church, and the Social Gospel, each of which sought to incarnate an alternative spiritual and political vision to the power plays of tyrants and moguls. We are not crusaders going off to war but prophets and healers, who envision a more perfect union, whose democratic principles promise liberty and justice for all.

The USA and the planet need a revival of a spiritually centered and socially active progressive Christian movement, claiming its role to heal and reconcile persons and nations, motivated by the power of love and not the love of power. Far from being monolithic in spirit and open to diversity of experience and perspective, American progressive Christians are challenged to embrace the wisdom of liberation, feminist, queer, ecojustice, indigenous and womanist theologies in broadening our circle of compassion and concern and creating pathways toward national transformation.

Vital progressive Christian faith must be nurtured and revitalized, not just for our own spiritual and congregational growth but to participate actively in God's quest to heal the earth. Progressive Christianity has a role in saving the world and this only will occur through claiming for ourselves and our congregations the dynamic interplay of vital theology, spirituality, prophetic faith, mission, and witness. Recognizing our own fallibility and the concrete limitations of history, we are nevertheless challenged to further the spiritual and moral arcs of history and claim our place humbly, in a pluralistic age, as God's companions in healing the world. We may even play a pivotal role in saving Christianity in the USA , including healing the spiritual lives of a growing number of persons who are leaving evangelical Christianity, disillusioned by its institutional abandonment of Jesus's teachings. We may even have a role in redeeming evangelical Christianity in the United States by calling it back to Jesus and challenging it to repent of its willingness to worship the idols of power, privilege, and prosperity rather than following God's vision of a Peaceable Realm embracing humankind in its wondrous variety and revealing Christ present in the vulnerable, troubled, persecuted, and oppressed "least of these."

Three years after the day of infamy and idolatry, and as the USA leans toward the 2024 election, there will be many more epiphanies revealing the promise as well as threat to our democracy and planetary wellbeing, calling us to decisions and actions related to democracy, human rights, global cooperation, climate change, and immigration. Progressive Christians will be called to sojourn on a heroic and holy adventure to save the soul of the nation and the planet and reclaim the heart of American Christianity. May we claim with humility the power of being companions in healing the soul of the nation and planet, and may we do this in companionship with seekers from the world's religious traditions as well as open spirited evangelical Christians, agnostics, and those who claim no faith. In this moment in history let us pray: "God, make us instruments of your peace, bringing peace on earth, beginning with us and expanding to fill the whole planet."

The Feast of Epiphany, January 6, 2024

Healing the American Spirit

Keep alert; stand firm in the faith; be courageous; be strong. (1 Corinthians 16:13)

To us all, to every nation,
There are moments to decide,
In the strife of truth and falsehood,
For the good or evil side.
Some great cause, God's new endeavor,
Offering us the bloom or blight,
And the choice goes on forever,
Twixt the darkness and the light.[1]

Today's progressive Christians are the children of the biblical prophets and healers, the Social Gospelers and the Freedom Riders. Our spiritual parents sought to be faithful to God in the complexities of politics and history. They knew that history reflects the interplay of divine call and human response in our daily decision-making and in the choices of leaders and institutions. They knew that the eternal God is also catalyst of change and adventure, "the steadfast love of the Lord never ceases, God's mercies

---

1 James Russell Lowell, "Once to Every Man and Nation," adapted by W. Garrett Horder.

never come to an end; they are new every morning; great is your faithfulness" (Lamentations 3:22-23). In our time, progressive Christians have come to realize that our response to God's faithful creativity shapes the course of our personal and national history just as it did during the time of Isaiah and Amos and Jesus and John the Baptist. Today's progressive Christians ground their faith in the holiness of each life. Created in the image of God, we are all kin, whether citizen or immigrant, or progressive or conservative, and deserve to embody God's aim at abundant life (John 10:10).

Our parents in the faith recognized the importance of personal responsibility and individual creativity in shaping history and responding to God's vision. As children of a relational trinitarian God, they affirmed that we are persons in community, and not isolated individuals, living in a world in which God's call and our response connects the solitude of mystical experience with the affairs of state, political leadership, realities of war and peace, and the price of food. Our biblical parents' prophetic vision enabled them to recognize that we are always on holy ground, confronted by God's vision in our homes and in the houses of government. Like them, we recognize that we are always on the way, humbly realizing that we are far from embodying God's vision of Shalom, in which the streets will be filled with joy and laughter and God's children will study war no more (Isaiah 2:4).

Our biblical and theological parents would have resonated with the Southern African word, *Ubuntu,* "I am because of you; we are because of one another," in their understanding of the interplay of spirituality and politics, and local and global healing. In the formation of persons and nations, God's vision is embodied or diminished as a result of our personal and institutional priorities, decisions, and actions.

Meeting the Moment

One encounter or event can transform a person or a nation or change the course of history. God calls not just "once to every person and nation," as James Russell Lowell asserts, but in every moment, God calls to us to be faithful to God's ever-evolving dream for the human adventure. That was true in David's palace and Solomon's Temple and also in Herod's court, the spiritual resistance of the Magi, and Joseph's dream and the flight of the Holy Family to Egypt. It is just as true now in our choice to respond with compassionate power toward those who subvert the message of Jesus to gain political power and perpetuate yesterday's injustices.

Each moment offers the choice of love or hate, and creation or destruction, and in each unfolding moment, the choice is ours to be creators or destroyers as individuals and citizens. There are pivotal moments in a nation's or person's history that may determine the rest of their lives or change the course of the future. As I noted in the preface to this book, one such pivotal moment of decision occurred on January 6, 2021, when hate-filled insurrectionists, motivated by a clear sense that they were supporting God's anointed leader sought secure his divine right to rule, regardless of consequences to human life or the USA democracy. Putting on what they believed to be the full armor of God, they stormed the Capitol, seeking to overthrow the United States government and take back their Christian country, turning back the clock to an imagined Christian America when women and persons of color knew their place, gay and lesbian persons were in the closet, and conservative "red tent" Christianity was the established religion.

The attack on January 6 was no accident nor was it an anomaly. Motivated by the same religious zealotry of the terrorists who sought to destroy the United States on September 11, 2001, these domestic terrorists believed that God was on their side, Trump was God's chosen president, and that regardless of the election results, securing Trump's victory, by whatever means, fulfilled God's manifest destiny for our nation. Inspired by the spirit of division, they believed that God had given them a mission to destroy the infidel, epitomized by a Congress and Vice-President seeking to be faithful to the Constitution. Marching to the Capitol, some carried signs proclaiming, "Jesus is my Savior. Trump is my President." Others gathered in prayer circles, asking for God's blessing of their chosen political Messiah and then rose up to annihilate anyone who stood in their way.

When they entered the Senate chambers, one group of insurrectionists gathered on the dais, where one insurrectionist proclaimed, "Jesus Christ, we invoke your name," to which the gathered men responded "Amen!" The prayer leader continued, entreating a "divine, omniscient, omnipotent and omnipresent creator God," thanking God for police officers who "allowed" them into the building to "exercise our rights, to allow us to send a message to all the tyrants, the communists and the globalists that this is our nation, not theirs."[2]

A few minutes before entering the Capitol, I suspect, many of these domestic terrorists may have followed their prayers for God's blessing with shouts of "Kill Mike Pence," as they charged gestapo-like toward the Capitol. Spiritually dead, denying Jesus' way of peace and reconciliation, they saw themselves as agents of retribution, marching around Jericho, with the same lust that excited Joshua's soldiers in their annihilation of everyone within Jericho's walls. While the USA democracy survived, the nation's soul was seriously traumatized and remains so as we move toward the 2024 election and beyond with racism, anti-Semitism, Islamophobia, and baldfaced lies about January 6 on the rise, much of these fueled by self-described evangelical Christians. These same insurrectionists and their leaders believe the path to the future is paved by the denial of obvious realities: racial injustice and slavery, climate change, science and the pandemic, and the fact of January 6 itself!

Contrary to authentic spirituality, which is always characterized by a sense of humility, these insurrectionists and conservative Christian activists are absolutely certain that their cause is blessed by God and that God blesses their American vision of individual-

2   Jack Jenkins, "The insurrectionists' Senate floor prayer highlights a curious Trumpian ecumenism." *Religion News Service*, February 25, 2021."
     (The insurrectionists' Senate floor prayer highlights a curious Trumpian ecumenism (religionnews.com)

ism, authoritarianism, theocracy, and planetary pillaging. Caught up in conspiracy theories and fantasies of America's golden age, they fail to realize that the nation needs the commitment to factuality, confession, and reparation as the prerequisites for healing its soul, and the birth of a spirit large enough to embrace contrasting views and diverse experiences in the quest for a "more perfect union" with "liberty and justice for all." They have exchanged the love of God for the devices and desires of their hearts, embodied in lust for this-worldly power. They have embraced wholeheartedly Jesus' temptations in the wilderness – power, comfort, and security – as the goals of their mission.

January 6 Lives On!

The events of January 6, 2021, were not a one-off but a reflection of a virus more deadly than COVID which has infected and continues to infect conservative and evangelical Christian congregations and their pastors and congregants with its veiled and sometimes explicit goal of "taking back America" to an earlier time of Christian cultural and political domination.

The same authoritarian and destructive spirit, albeit "kinder and gentler" in demeanor, was at work, nearly three years later, when Christian fundamentalist Mike Johnson ascended to the Speaker of the House, and in his inaugural speech asserted that "I believe that scripture, the Bible is very clear that God is the one that raises up those in authority. He raised up each of you, all of us, and I believe that God has ordained and allowed each one of us to be brought here for this specific moment in this time." Another election-denier and January 6-minimizer, Johnson embraced his own God-ordained authority, while omitting the irony that God had also – according to his stated belief in the divine choice of leadership – ordained President Joe Biden and his fellow Democratic party representatives as well! When asked about what guides his life, Johnson responded, "I am a Bible-believing Christian. Someone asked me today in the media, they said, 'People are curious, what does Mike Johnson think about any issue under the sun?' I said, 'Well, go pick up a Bible off your shelf and read it.' That's my worldview." Of course, it is reasonable to ask, based on his vision of America, which parts of the Bible is he reading and what scriptures has he discarded. Is his Bible a holy bible embracing the whole earth or an excuse for Christian imperialism and the suppression of diversity?

Guided by his claim that he is guided by the biblical worldview and God's revelation that he is the Moses to lead us across troubled waters, one of Johnson's first acts was to rush through symbolic bills radically decreasing funding of the Environmental Protection Agency and National Parks Service, with the goal of limiting environmental restrictions and promoting the use of fossil fuels, despite the clear scientific evidence of the positive impact of environmental regulations in responding global climate, air and water quality, and the overall physical health of the nation.[3] A believer in the imminent Second Coming of Jesus, I suspect Johnson thinks that if Jesus is coming soon – a dubious ethical position with little scriptural support – there is no reason to care for the planet or protect its wilderness places. Unstated is the belief that in the meantime, as we wait for Jesus' "imminent" return, we can fill our coffers, attack the aspirations toward equality of persons of color, immigrants, and the LGBTQ+ community, and support unrestrained capitalism.

Johnson's Christian exceptionalism is not unique among today's evangelical Christians and Trump supporters. As a matter of fact, it is the theological and political norm for many of today's conservative Christians. The cocktail of authoritarian Christianity, Second Coming anticipation, and theological absolutism jeopardizes the soul of the nation, puts at risk anyone who walks to the beat of a different drummer and wreaks havoc on planetary well-being. Motivated by their thin-skinned, partisan, and violent deity's chosen political messenger's goal of "retribution," such

---

3   Priest Issues 'Red Flag' Warning About Mike Johnson Remarks (news-week.com), February 8, 2024.

Christian absolutists threaten to destroy anyone who stands in the way of their dream of establishing an authoritarian Christian state in which Christians are in control and everyone knows their divinely ordained place as subservient, closeted, and on the sidelines of history. Their opponents are described as "vermin" whose existence "poisons" the purity of the nation, who must be silenced, rounded up, or exterminated to bring about God's reign in the United States. They are willing to destroy the nation and put the planet at risk to achieve their fantasy of a Christian theocracy.

The Personal is Political and the Political is Personal

North American theologian Reinhold Niebuhr once noted the irony that some of the most generous persons in one-on-one interpersonal relationships are mysteriously transformed into the most violent and authoritarian zealots when they align themselves with ideologies, movements, and institutions, whether governmental or religious. We need only look at the contrast between Southern hospitality and Jim Crow laws and German sophistication and Nazism. There is both strength and violence in numbers! Otherwise mild mannered conservative Christians contemplate and on occasion do the most violent and destructive things when they experience the illusory power of groupthink. Otherwise, privileged people and members of a privileged faith community see themselves and their congregations as martyrs oppressed by pluralism, the gay agenda, drag queens, public schools, vaccines, face masks, and black lives matter. The legal indictments levied against the chosen political Messiah are identified with Jesus' suffering on the Cross and their own reduced status in a pluralistic society.

I am sure that if your car was broken down on the side of the road outside of Washington DC in the early hours of January 6, many of the soon-to-be insurrectionists would have stopped to lend a hand, provided you didn't have a Biden/Harris, rainbow, or marriage equality sticker on your bumper or were a person of color. Many are decent and caring people in their individual lives until they are called to invoke theological and political ideologies in the public sphere. They sing "Jesus loves me, this I know" and also embrace the image of a militant Jesus who leads their crusade against premarital sex among teenagers, abortion, and drag queens as if these are the most consequential ethical issues of our times or, frankly, even would have mattered to Jesus of Nazareth. They talk about love for their neighbor until they show up at a MAGA event and clap wildly to calls to exterminate the left-wing vermin and round up immigrants, described as thugs and rapists. They want freedom to practice their brand of Christianity while threatening to place limitations on everyone else's religious freedoms. They worry about crime in metropolitan areas and oppose any restrictions of firearms.

When provoked by the vitriolic rhetoric of their divine-ly anointed politicians and pastors – in a blink of an eye, like the Incredible Hulk, otherwise benign Christians begin to rage against gays, drag queens, immigrant thugs, abortion providers, and progressive politicians and tree huggers as God's enemies, their oppressors, and the ruination of our society.[4] Conservative and self-styled evangelical Christians do good works. Many of their churches have programs that feed the hungry, respond to substance use addiction, and help forgotten children. But, the political policies they support undermine their good works and often harm the people they claim to help.

Our conservative Christian kin love the creedal Christ, before whom every knee must bow or be forced to bow in order to receive salvation, but marginalize Jesus' message of peace, reconciliation, forgiveness, and love of enemies central to the Sermon on the Mount and the prophets who shaped Jesus' spirituality. Jesus' forgiveness of enemies, welcome of outcasts and foreigners, and emphasis on sacrificial living is too impractical – indeed, too wimpy - for governance, and must be discarded as an unaccept-

---

4   Trump Echoes Hitler, Threatens to Rid America of 'Vermin' from Within (msn.com)

able check on free market capitalism. They believe that God needs fighters, not lovers, in the crusade for a truly Christian America!

It Can Happen Here!

The old-style revivalist preachers of my childhood Baptist church often presented the bad news of sin, before the good news of salvation! They wanted their listeners to wake up to the temptations of the "evil one" and the dangers of the wide path of immorality and idolatry. In the spirit of the Baptist revival preachers, who visited our small-town church each summer, I also began with the bad news of white Christian nationalism and conservative Christian theocracy as a prelude to the good news that progressive Christians can respond to a twenty-first century altar call and become a vital force in moving our nation forward toward a diverse, welcoming, and justice-seeking "more perfect union." While not calling for a narrow view of salvation or monolithic national revival and recognizing that there is still hope for repentance in conservative Christianity, I believe that we need to recognize the dangers of authoritarian Christianity and our equally dangerous complacency as progressive Christians in relationship to threats to democracy, free speech, climate, and justice for humankind in all its diversity.

While my critique of conservative Christian and white nationalism is harsh, I am a realist, reporting the facts as I witness them from rallies, pulpits, and media interviews and posts. I am calling on my progressive and authentically evangelical Christian kin to wake up to their role in healing the nation and planet.[5]

Authoritarian populism, much of it religiously inspired, is on the rise in democratic nations, from Hungary to India and the United States to Israel. In many ways, the situation in the USA resembles 1930's Germany, as a large segment of our nation wants

5   Tim Alberta, an evangelical Christian, well documents the idolatry in today's USA conservative Christianity. Tim Alberta, *The Kingdom, The Power, and the Glory: American Evangelicals in an Age of Extremism* (New York: Harper, 2023)

a strong man, who erects clear an impregnable wall separating in-
siders and outsiders, to solve their problems and ensure their privilege rather than accept the risks of freedom and democracy. The
threat to democracy and the planet is real. A nation dominated by
Christian nationalists threatens the survival of democracy, not to
mention the lives of political opponents, persons of color, immigrants, and members of the LGBTQ+ community, through its authoritarianism and puts the planet in peril through its adherence
to the dangerous cocktail of free market economics and Second
Coming theology. Today's white Christian nationalists have traded, if not besmirched irreparably, the name "evangelical," replac-
ing a personal relationship with Jesus, issuing in acts of mercy and
compassion, with adherence to the gods of power and control, and
nation and privilege.

The Path of Prophetic Challenge and Healing

As I outline the dangers of authoritarian religion, my goal is
not to demonize, dehumanize, or denigrate those whom I see as
threats to the soul of the nation. Grounded in our belief in God's
graceful and all-encompassing love, the goal of healing the nation
must embrace the "lost" sheep of authoritarian Christianity as well
as those within the fold of progressive Christianity, our "enemies"
as well as our friends!

Progressive Christians also need a "come to Jesus" moment.
We need to claim our vocation to heal the soul of the nation
through a robust commitment to theological reflection, spiritual formation, and practical social action. I want to be clear that
progressive Christians are not necessarily superior in individual
morality or interpersonal relationships. Nor are progressive Christians immune from the fear-based decision-making that motivates
those whose politics and religion we challenge. I also recognize
that the spirit of incivility, hate, and demonization can infect progressive politics, as it has recently in the vitriol by certain ideo-

logical progressives aimed at Jewish Americans and Jewish college students during the Israeli-Hamas war.

While there are psychological and sociological explanations of the rise of authoritarian movements and the unquestioned support of morally dubious and anti-democratic leaders, the main justification given by conservative Christians for their commitment to authoritarian politics and religion is theological: we have the truth and you don't, we are chosen and you aren't, we are saved and you are lost, God speaks to us and not you, only we can save the nation, and all other voices threaten our way of life and must be silenced in the ballot box and school boards we or eliminated altogether. To the doctrinal and ideological gatekeepers, pluralism is a fall from grace and a threat to Christianity. Progressive open-spiritedness, commitment to pluralism, and hospitality to strangers is heretical and apostate, perverting the message of their American Jesus. Only orthodoxy and uniformity of doctrine, inspiring a return to traditional American values, is God's intended path to salvation. Indeed, as is the case with the insurrectionists and climate deniers, adherents to this viewpoint would rather destroy democracy and the planet than question their world views, compromise to make pragmatic political decisions, or sacrifice to share the prerogatives of power and privilege. That many of the most ardent supporters of nationalist, racist, anti-science, and anti-democracy perspectives claim to be Christian, and are willing to put on the whole armor of God to go to join the crusade against the infidel, puts the future of Jesus' message, the dream of democracy, and the wellbeing of the planet at risk.

In this context, the call is clear: progressive Christians and allies of all faiths or no religious tradition must "rise and shine" and follow God's all-revealing and all-encompassing light. We must confront threats to our faith, nation, and planet, but we must equally be guided by the power of love and inspired by the quest for prophetic healing, and the emergence of a world that embraces both citizen and immigrant, MAGA adherent and Black Lives Matter protester, industrialist and environmentalist. The future belongs to prophetic healers, who seek to embody God's dream of Shalom, the Peaceable Realm, in politics, economics, and relationships.

Wake Up Progressives!

The future of Christianity in the northern hemisphere is in doubt, and much of it is the result of the Christianity we present to the world. Polls suggest that young people want little to do with authoritarian, backward-looking, and narrow-minded religion, whether Christian, Muslim, or Jewish, or any other tradition. They often naively assume that all Christians are anti-LGBTQ+, anti-science, anti-democracy, anti-diversity, anti-woman, anti-environment, and intolerant and authoritarian. According to public opinion research, a growing number of USA citizens are afraid of evangelical Christians today, fearing physical attacks, ostracism and bullying, and elimination of hard-fought civil liberties. Sadly, their fears are justified: among a sizeable group of self-described evangelical Christians, based on their political affiliation, images of God and Christ are often coopted by and connected with the most divisive and narrow-minded visions of reality such that a person's view of climate change, social welfare programs, and the 2020 election pretty much reveals everything you need to know about their Jesus! And when seeing Jesus being trumpeted by many politically and theologically conservative Christians, seekers and youth find more hope for salvation in agnosticism and claiming the title "none of the above" than in the Jesus of evangelical Christianity.

The prophet Ezekiel once had a vision of dry bones in a valley, and asked "Can these bones – the bones of a broken and dying nation - live?" The same question can be asked of America, "Can these broken bones be healed? Can the ruptures in our nation, going back to 1619, be mended in such a way that our nation can embrace diversity and disagreement without violence and division? Can we seek to heal the soul of the nation, so that we can balance healthy patriotism with world loyalty?" We might ask similar questions of members of our own progressive Christian congregations. "Can we rise up strong, vital, compassionate, and politically powerful in our time of chaos and crisis?"

In this time of rising white conservative Christian nationalism, progressive Christians are challenged to wake up, put on the armor of light and spirit of healing, and present a robust alternative vision to promote national and planetary healing which will move our nation forward and also serve as a firewall to protect the nation and planet in response to the worst angels of their conservative Christian kin's quest for political power. We must challenge injustice and theocratic public policy while recognizing the holiness, the image of God, in those whose views we challenge.

Progressive Christianity needs healing, too! We need God's breath to resuscitate our dry bones and vitalize our congregations. We need illumination and energy to discern how to navigate the political waters with wisdom and compassion. Progressive Christians need to wake up to the peril of our times, deepen their spiritual practices and theological reflection, and articulate a prophetic spirituality that heals rather divides. At such a time as this, we must strengthen our spirits and voices in the political and planetary sphere in ways that are humble, inclusive, hospitable, and that seek prophetic healing and not the destruction of our opponents. Even when we must challenge what we believe to be dangerous theologies and theological involvements in politics by our fellow Christians, we are called to seek reconciliation rather than destruction. We are challenged to be motivated by the vision of a "more perfect union" and a just and sustainable planet, and not our fears of this-worldly national and political this-apocalypse.

The time may be short for our nation, and for the planet, and we may reach a point of no return in terms of planetary climate change and the preservation of democracy, but in the meantime, we must be hopeful and joyful proponents of God's vision of Shalom. We must do the work placed before us to heal the earth, regardless of what the future brings. We are called to be faithful even if we are uncertain of the success of our endeavors.

We can be both humble and persistent, and open-spirited and decisive. We can recognize, without being daunted by, the limitations of our own positions as we challenge others and train our eyes to see God's presence in places that we deem it is most defaced. We must act for ecological justice and human rights, inspired by the affirmation that the world is healed one act at a time and that our vocation is to join with God in repairing the world.

Theology Matters and Spirituality Transforms: Confronting Theologies of Death and Division

Theology matters! Spiritual practices matter! Faith revealed in acts of healing and hospitality one on one and in the political and planetary sphere matters! Toxic and authoritarian theologies inspire authoritarian, scorched earth, and binary political action. Toxic and authoritarian theologies cannot abide with otherness and multiplicity. From the point of view of authoritarian religion, whether in the fourth, twelfth, or twenty-first century, the infidel must be crushed, because if the infidel is correct at any point, the certainty necessary for authoritarian and fundamentalist faith to flourish collapses.

"The Bible says it, I believe it, that settles it!" – the mantra of conservative Christianity – easily morphs into a politician shouting "I am your retribution," and the promotion of heresy trials, inquisitions, crusades, and persecutions not to mention banning books and demonizing immigrants and persons of color.

Let me repeat: an authoritarian God, violent, thin-skinned, and narcissistic in nature, inspires an equally thin-skinned, narcissistic and domineering religion and politics. Followers of the authoritarian God assert that there is only "one way" to salvation and that is our way. There is only one true patriotism and that is our white nationalism.

In this time of binary and aggressive politics and religion, we must be theologically insightful and astute. Progressives must present an alternative vision of God and the world. We must be prophetic healers and compassionate and prayerful protesters. While I will provide a more detailed robust theological vision later in this text, the contours of a humble, yet powerful vision of God, inspiring an equally powerful prophetic spirituality and politics involve reclaiming the power of affirmative, lively, and inclusive faith, with affirmations such as:

» God is love and God's love embraces everyone, friend and foe.

» God loves the world and that means the non-human as well as human world.

» God reveals Godself to everyone in every culture.

» God's moral and spirit arc aim toward beauty, justice, inclusion, and healing the planet.

» God is the inspiration of social transformation and planetary healing.

» God is the energy behind the processes of planetary and political evolution.

» God loves diversity and seeks to join unity and diversity in the creation of just societies.

» God's image is the deepest reality of every human and is found in the non-human world as well.

» God's revelation is broadcast generously, such that diversity of opinion is an opportunity for growth, not persecution.

» God wants us to be God's partners in healing the world.

» God's moves in history not toward a Second Coming, or apocalyptic catastrophe, but to a "Millisecond Coming," revealed in every encounter and person.

» Faithfulness to God takes us beyond individualism and self-interest, sect and nation, to world loyalty.

» History is open-ended and what we do shapes the historical process toward creation or destruction.

»   God needs us to embody God's vision in the world. What we do matters to God, the world, and the future of our planet.

Whereas authoritarian theology is motivated by the love of power, the need to control, and the suppression of conflicting experiences and opinions, healthy theology is inspired by the power of love and the unity of person and community, embracing a variety of religious and political perspectives, and diverse races, cultures, and sexual expressions, for the common good. God loves diversity and honors relationships. The Holy Trinity embodies pluralism and parents forth a diverse universe, planet, and human race.

Yes, theology matters, and progressives need to be bold in our theology. We cannot let our affirmation of pluralism paralyze us. We must honor diverse points of view, seek common cause with persons of different faiths and political perspectives, as a reflection of our bold world affirming theology. We must become actors on the national and world stage in the spirit of our Social Gospel parents of the twentieth century.

I believe that a well-articulated holistic progressive theology will inspire, and deepen peoples' spiritual lives, and also motivate persons to personal and political responsibility and transform persons and societies. Lively and robust progressive theology and spiritually grounded political practice will serve as a firewall to lessen the impact of authoritarian theologies and politics. More than that, it will provide people with something to believe in, a this-worldly faith to affirm, and a vision of our vocation as God's companions in healing the world.

I realize that although most progressive Christians, including myself, would like to sit on the sidelines, trusting the wisdom of the American people and good heartedness of our Christian kin to make the right decisions, this won't happen unless we become actors and agents in shaping the future of democracy and the planet. As a pastor, university chaplain and professor, and seminary professor for over forty years, I prefer contemplation and the leisure of scholarship and writing to political involvement. But, theology has always been political. Each of us in our unique way must promote the moral and spiritual arcs of history, whether in teaching, writing, and preaching, protest and calls to representatives, town meetings, political volunteerism, advocacy for marginalized and persecuted people, and the repair of past injustices. In our time of national and international upheaval, the Word made flesh in occupied Bethlehem two thousand years ago challenges us to a politics of compassion, creativity, community, caring, and challenge. The Incarnate One challenges our churches to come alive spiritually and politically so they can be a force for healing and social transformation, loving this earth and trusting God's guidance as God's companions in healing the planet.

Nourishing a Robust and Activist Progressive Spirit

The future of progressive Christianity as a force for national and planetary transformation is grounded in the interplay of theology and spirituality. We need to embrace, without polarization, our identity as reflections of God's light of the world and let our light shine in acts of prophetic and planetary healing aimed at embracing friend and foe, and kin and stranger, alike. We need as, Amanda Gorman says, following Jesus' affirmation, to see the light and then be the light, bringing forth the light in others as we kindle our own inner light. Accordingly, each chapter concludes with a spiritual practice to nurture a robust and activist progressive spirit.

Asking for Guidance. In Jesus' manifesto on spirituality and ethics, the Sermon on the Mount, Jesus counsels his followers and us to "ask, seek, and knock." Similarly, in his social gospel classic, *In His Steps,* Charles Sheldon challenges those who seek to be faithful to Jesus' ethical mission to ask "what would Jesus do?" whenever they are confronted with an ethical, interpersonal, or political decision. In that spirit, as you ponder your responsibility as a citizen, make it a habit to ask for divine guidance. As you watch the news or listen to the radio, let the headlines and feature stories call you to prayer for the persons involved and for guidance in fulfilling your responsibility to be an agent of God's prophetic and planetary healing.

As I write this text, in the winter of 2023 and 2024, Israel and Hamas are in the midst of a catastrophic military conflict in which thousands of innocent persons, including children have been casualties. My prayer has been, "what am I called to do as a USA citizen?" who cannot control the actions of a foreign government. So far, I have been led to contact my Senators on several occasions to encourage the USA to work toward a ceasefire between the warring parties. I have been on the lookout for opportunities to be allies with both Muslim and Jewish kin who may experience harassment at public places. I take a little longer at the service station or walk more slowly when I see a woman in a hijab or my Jewish neighbors walking to Temple on Saturday, attentive to any threats they may receive, and ready to stand non-violently beside them.

As a result of our economic and political privilege, none of us are innocent bystanders in an interdependent world. Even though we are not political decision-makers, we can regularly challenge our political leaders to pursue justice and peace. We can be involved in political meetings, protests, and campaigns in quest for Shalom, knowing that even our smallest actions can further the spiritual and moral arcs of the universe. Let us pray for God's guidance in our personal and political lives. Let us ask God to lead us in embodying the way of life and love for ourselves, those we love, the nation, and the planet.

Seeing the Light

John's Gospel proclaims that "the true light, which enlightens everyone, was coming into the world." (John 1:9) Genesis 1:26 proclaims that every human is created in the likeness, or image, of the Divine. Accordingly, there is something of God in everyone, an inner light, as the Quakers assert. God's light shines in Palestinian and Israeli children, in MAGA supporters and political progressives, in descendants of the Mayflower and Central American families seeking asylum. Look for the light in every person, pray for those who are strangers and opponents, as you seek justice and planetary healing.

In that spirit, as you watch the news or participate in political action, look for the light in yourself and let your light shine. (Matthew 5:14-16) Let Jesus' light flow in and through you to the world. In this time of divisiveness, polarization, and demonization of opponents, look for the light – God's presence – in those with whom you disagree. See the hidden light in perpetrators of injustice and inciters of violence. Seeing the light in your political opponents and praying for their wellbeing enables you to challenge their positions, protest their policies, and work to elect alternative candidates, without polarizing or demonizing. We can choose to live by love and not fear in our individual and political lives.

Our most ardent protests should be conditioned by Jesus' counsel to his disciples, facing the violent Roman oppression of first century Judea, and to us as we seek a "more perfect union" in the context of prevaricators of falsehood and agents of incivility. "But I say to you: Love your enemies and pray for those who persecute you, so that you may be children of your Father in heaven, for he makes his sun rise on the evil and on the good and sends rain on the righteous and on the unrighteous" (Matthew 5:44-45). Our calling is to "be perfect, therefore, as God our Parent is perfect," that is, to be persons of stature and inclusiveness, whose love embraces friend and foe alike. We should take to heart a statement I read on Facebook, "the true test of Christianity isn't just loving Jesus, it is loving Judas!" Our salvation, and the salvation of our planet, depends on each of us discovering God's light in ourselves and seeing God's light in our political allies and opponents (Matthew 5:48). We can picket and pray, and protest and promote community, grounded in our commitment to see Christ in the least of these as well as those whose policies and beliefs promote injustice, incivility, and insurrection.

HERE WE ARE, SEND US!

*In the year that King Uzziah died, I saw the Lord
sitting on a throne, high and lofty, and the hem of his
robe filled the temple. Seraphs were in attendance above
him; each had six wings: with two they covered their faces,
and with two they covered their feet, and with two they
flew. And one called to another and said,*

> *"Holy, holy, holy is the LORD of hosts;
> the whole earth is full of his glory." ...*

*And I said, "Woe is me! I am lost, for I am a man of
unclean lips, and I live among a people of unclean lips, yet
my eyes have seen the King, the LORD of hosts!" ... Then I
heard the voice of the Lord saying, "Whom shall I send,
and who will go for us?" And I said, "Here am I; send me!"*

(Isaiah 6:1-3, 5, 8)

*I don't know Who – or what – put the question. I
don't know when it was put. I don't even remember answering. But at some moment I did answer Yes to Someone – or something – and from that hour I was certain
that existence is meaningful and, that, therefore, my life,
in self-surrender, had a goal. From that moment I have*

known what it means "not to look back" and "to take no
thought for the morrow."[6]

I want to begin this section on God's call to a robust progressive Christianity with a confession or is it an assertion? I do
not believe in a databable and preordained Second Coming. While
such "left behind" theology has become orthodoxy in many conservative and evangelical Christian circles, including many of the
most powerful Republicans in the USA Congress, I think the
relatively recent nineteenth century notion that Jesus will come
in our lifetime to rapture the saints is one of the greatest hoaxes
perpetrated on Christianity and one of the most dangerous doctrinal perspectives not only because it requires all sorts of biblical
gymnastics to make theological and spiritual sense of it and puts
a minor theme in scripture at center stage but also insofar as it:
1) turns our attention from earth to heaven and from communal healing to individual salvation, 2) falsely separates the saved
and unsaved, 3) demonizes our opponents as eternally lost, and
4) assumes that God's rescue operation is restricted to a favored
few chosen believers. It also assumes that God is on the outside of
our world and will only intervene supernaturally to save the true
believers while the rest of the world is destroyed, in part due to
God's own vindictiveness.

Doctrines of the Second Coming encourage hopelessness and
pessimism about history, turn our attention to the eternal and
away from history, and promote binary and individualistic no-
tions of salvation in which only the true believers are saved while
the infidels will experience the wrath of God. God the destroyer
becomes the primary model of scorched earth politics and ethics.
For those awaiting the rapture, the bad news is good news. War,
especially in the Middle East, is a sign of the imminence of the
Second Coming, and environmental upheaval alerts us to earth's
ultimate destruction. There is no use trying to save the earth. Just

---

6   Dag Hammarskjold, *Markings* (New York: Knopf), 1964.

trust Jesus and make money in the meantime! The earth is living on borrowed time, so why bother to protect the environment.

In contrast to world-denying theology, I affirm the Millisecond Coming of Christ, described by Jesus in Matthew 25:31-46. God doesn't come just once into our lives but is constantly calling us to "follow Christ" embodied in Jesus' vocation to heal the sick, free the captives, liberate the oppressed, feed the hungry, and midwife God's vision of Shalom by our personal and political commitments. God is found in the "least of these" now in the joys and sorrows of this world, and not in some separate reality. We don't need to substitute an imagined carefree future populated by "saved" people just like ourselves for the real presence of God in our time and place in all its complexity, chaos, and beauty. This world matters to God, and it should matter to us. God's love is universal, and so should ours. God loves the here and now in all its earthiness and wants us to be as incarnate in our world as change agents as Jesus was in Judea. God's focus for us now is this lifetime and not some future afterlife and this lifetime should be our focus, too. If we are in sync with God's vision, eternity will take care of itself!

In the midst of a national crisis, not unlike our own, in which the future of the realm is in doubt, Isaiah encounters the living God and is forever transformed. Mysticism leads to mission. Humbled by his encounter with the God of the universe in contrast to his own sinful and finite humanity, Isaiah hears God's call for a messenger to do what God can't do without Isaiah's partnership: call the nation's leaders to align themselves with God's vision, turn to God's way, and establish justice in the nation. In a dramatic moment, Isaiah hears the voice of God addressed directly to him, "Whom shall I send" to bring the nation back to God's ways. Overcoming his sense of sinfulness and insignificance, Isaiah stammers, "Here am I, send me."

Another privileged person, Queen Esther embraces her destiny to be her people's savior, "for just such a time as this." While she wants to stay on the sidelines and let others do the work of saving her people, she is challenged by her relative Mordecai's words and chooses to lead a counteroffensive against those who would commit genocide against the Jewish people. In such mystical moments, whether dramatic or gradual, we say "yes" to God's call to become God's companions in healing the world. United Nations Secretary General Dag Hammarskjold hears a question, whose Source is unknown, and in responding affirmatively finds direction and meaning to his life and claims his role as peacemaker in a troubled world.

I believe that individual Christians and progressive Christianity as a movement are called to become agents in God's quest to heal the world and the soul of our nation. The God of the Universe needs companions, like Isaiah, Esther, Mary of Nazareth, Saul (Paul) of Tarsus, Mahatma Gandhi, Martin Luther King, Fannie Lou Hamer, Oscar Romero, Dorothy Day, and Mother (Saint) Teresa to push the moral and spiritual arcs of history forward and to call our respective nations to become agents of justice. The God of the Universe needs you and your congregation! You matter and your congregation matters in God's quest for global healing. God needs you and your congregation to embody prophetic healing in our time. The call of God may not be dramatic, but it is given moment by moment in our personal encounters, inspirations and insights, and the affairs of history.

Contemplative activists such as Isaiah, Esther, and Dag Hammarskjold as well as today's politically involved mystics encounter the Living God and that encounter energizes and empowers them to transform the world. Encountering the Living God encourages activity, not passivity, and solidarity, not isolation. As the Spanish mystic Teresa of Avila proclaims:

> Christ has no body now but yours. No hands, no feet on earth but yours. Yours are the eyes through which he looks compassion on this world. Yours are the feet with which he walks to do good. Yours are the hands through which he blesses all the world. Yours are the hands, yours are the feet, yours

are the eyes, you are his body. Christ has no body now on earth but yours.

We matter to God. Our efforts matter to God. Committed to God's vision, we can do great things to heal the soul of the nation and save the planet.

Partnering with God!

God is constantly calling us in the micro and macro events of our lives. God's call always joins time and eternity, this moment and the horizons of Shalom. In real time and concrete historical events, God invites us to be partners in God's vision of justice in this world. God's aim in the universe is toward beauty and wholeness for all creation, and this aim at abundant life is offered to us and the world one moment at a time. Each moment can be a tipping point from death to life and chaos to creativity for persons and nations.

The living God takes flesh in the concrete realities of an oppressed land. As African American mystic Howard Thurman notes, Jesus never spent a moment as a free person. He lived under the thumb of Roman oppressors and their Judean religious and political minions. He also felt the vice grip of religious legalism and its division of the world into righteous and sinful, clean and unclean, and welcomed and excluded. Jesus' ministry was aimed at healing and empowering concrete persons to experience and convey God's abundant life through acts of faithful hospitality and inclusion. A spiritual child of the prophets, without political power, Jesus inspires those who follow him to live by a different set of values than the unjust social order whether in occupied first century Judea or powerful twenty-first century United States. Jesus envisioned the Beloved Community, the Realm of Shalom, in his time and challenges us to promote Beloved Community here on earth in the scrum of economics, politics, and earth care.

The early church also lived under the thumb of Roman oppression. Although the early Jesus movement lacked the power and social standing to challenge the Empire, they chose to live by a different way of life and a different set of values than the Empire: sharing their possessions, ensuring everyone had adequate support, promoting the leadership of women, choosing peace over war, and welcoming diversity. They had no political power and did not envision a domineering theocracy and thus did not create a political philosophy. But in the formation of their communities, they embodied the interplay of generosity, hospitality, unity, and diversity necessary for the achievement of justice in states and nations. That is also our calling: to live by the values of community, generosity, and hospitality in our congregations and political involvement. To have, as Martin Luther King counsels, the strength to love and the resilience to challenge injustice while seeking the spiritual well-being of its perpetrators.

Our call for just such a time as ours is also to be prophets and healers – prophetic healers – who challenge injustice, promote freedom, and further inclusion while seeing God's presence in those whom we oppose. We are challenged as progressive Christians to present an alternative reality to violence, exclusion, consumerism, demagoguery, and ecological destruction. We are called to use our power with love and privilege with sacrifice to expand the circles of abundant life and wholeness to embrace the stranger as well as kin.

In a way that includes all people, the future belongs to the prophets and not to power hungry politicians. God's vision calls for multipliers and not diminishers and welcomers and not excluders. The generous not the fearful. They are the apostles of love and hospitality, not the fomenters of hate and incivility and earthly pilgrims who seek God's realm rather than Caesar's empire. The calling of progressive Christianity is to join personal spiritual transformation with institutional and national transformation. The personal is the political, and the political calls forth our personal vocation to heal the nation and the world.

God has the whole world in God's hands, as the spiritual proclaims, and God has given us the responsibility to be stewards of creation and shepherds of humankind. Our calling is to model our lives after the Loving and Healing God, the Great Empath, and Most Moved Mover, and not the gods of vindictiveness and violence. The future is in God's hands, and nothing can separate us from the love of God in Christ Jesus our Savior. (Romans 8:38-39) Trusting the future, we can focus on one world at a time, as Thoreau averred on his deathbed, partnering with God to heal the earth and its peoples and trusting God to handle everlasting life.

Nurturing a Robust and Activist Progressive Spirit

All creation is called forth by God's loving imagination. Each moment is a "thin place," as Celtic spiritual guides assert, transparent to God's vision for just such a time as this. Although God's call goes on moment by moment, and millisecond by millisecond, God's call is always invitational, and never coercive. The quality of our response is shaped by our openness to the divine. The following practices can awaken us to God's call in our lives and energize us to embody God's call in our personal relationships and community.

Living with the Call Stories and Discovering that You are a Mystic. In First or Native American communities, it is common for young persons to "cry for a vision" that will guide their lives and shape their identities. As progressive Christians and congregations, we need to go on vision quests to discern our vocation in the chaos of North American politics. Jesus describes this call, as I noted in the first chapter, in terms of asking, seeking, and knocking in relationship to embodying God's realm in our lives. The scriptures provide us with a multitude of call stories. God's call can come to anyone at any time. Young Samuel hears God speaking in the night. Uncertain of the source of the voice, he consults his mentor, the priest Eli, who eventually identifies the nocturnal voice as God. He advises his young student to listen and respond. When the voice comes again, Samuel responds with an open spirit.

Now the LORD came and stood there, calling as before, "Samuel! Samuel!" And Samuel said, "Speak, for your servant is listening. (1 Samuel 3:10, see 1 Samuel 3:1-10)

Hopeless, following the crucifixion of Jesus, Mary of Magdala comes to the Garden, and confuses the Risen Jesus for a gardener until he calls her name.

> Jesus said to her, "Mary!" She turned and said to him in Hebrew, "Rabbouni!" (which means Teacher). Jesus said to her, "Do not touch me, because I have not yet ascended to the Father. But go to my brothers and say to them, 'I am ascending to my Father and your Father, to my God and your God.'" Mary Magdalene went and announced to the disciples, "I have seen the Lord," and she told them that he had said these things to her. (John 20:17-18, see John 20:11-18)

Encounters with God inspire action. Jesus comforts us and then challenges us with a vision for service. Mysticism leads to world transforming mission, whether we speak of Samuel and Mary, or Peter and Paul, or the first Pentecost. God is still speaking, God's call is still sounding, but we must prepare to hear God's call and then embrace it in our own unique time and place and with our own unique gifts and social location.

You may not think of yourself as a mystic. But, God is calling you in the daily and sometimes dull events of your life. There is something of God in you, whether or not you notice it. Spiritual practices can awaken you to God's voice and your vocation. In this practice, follow in the spirit of Holy Reading or Lectio Divina, focusing on the calls of Samuel and Mary respectively, noted above, on two successive days by:

1) Beginning with a time of silence and prayerful openness to God.
2) Reading the scripture twice, pausing between each reading and following the second reading.
3) Listen for a word or image that comes to you in the

course of your meditation.

4) Consider prayerfully the word or image that comes to you, asking for its meaning in your life.

5) Ask God how this inspiration might relate to your lifestyle, relationships, or citizenship and political involvement.

6) Give thanks for God's inspiration in your life and pray to embody God's guidance in your personal life and citizenship.

7) Look for insights related to your experience throughout the day and as you watch the news or read news feeds or the newspaper.

8) When insights occur, ask for God's guidance in terms of living out your faith in your relationships and in the public sphere.

This spiritual practice awakens us and our congregations to God's "still, small voice" whether in your personal life or citizenship, alerting us to the reality that the world is saved one moment and action at a time.

3

HEALING OURSELVES
AND OUR POLITICS

*I have come that they might have life, and have it
abundantly.* (John 10:10)

This text is about healing and healing relates to every aspect
of our lives: The healing of progressive open-spirited Christianity,
of our evangelical Christian kin, and the healing of our nation
and the planet. The viruses of racism, dictatorship, incivility, mil-
itarism, and ecocide threaten our well-being, and we must find an
antidote and alternative vision of theological, spiritual, national,
and planetary health. At this moment in time, we progressives
need to develop our theological reflection and spiritual practices
in ways that will transform our congregations, communities, and
the earth. Healing involves the experience of abundant life not
just for us but for all creation: fully alive humanity, and food, shel-
ter, healthcare, education, and love enough for everyone. I believe
that a hopeful future for our nation and planet results from the
healthy and life-changing interplay of theological visions, spiritual
practices, and prophetic political involvement at the personal and
communal levels.

Progressive Christians need to reclaim and expand the healing ministry of Jesus for a scientific and pluralistic age. We have too long let supernaturalist images of healing prevent us from taking Jesus' healings seriously. We have also been discouraged by Christian preachers who connect sin with sickness and counsel congregants that if they only have enough faith, God will cure their diseases and fill their pockets with money. In contrast to such simplistic and transactional understandings of healing, Jesus' healings encompassed body, mind, and spirit in all their complexity. They also embraced relationships and by implication the social order. Jesus did not blame the victim, nor did he connect God's power with sickness or poverty. While we do not need to take the healing stories literally and need to adapt them according to our current medical knowledge, we must take them seriously as a manifestation of God's aim at wholeness moving through all things personal and institutional. We also must understand Jesus' healings in light of the growing evidence that our attitudes, lifestyle, religious practices, and relationships are factors in health and illness.

Healing was at the heart of Jesus' vision of the kingdom, or kindom, of God. Jesus invited his followers to pray "thy kingdom come; thy will be done on earth as it is in heaven." God's heavenly spiritual and moral vision was intended to become the daily reality of persons and nations. We can be heavenly minded and earthly good. Rooted in God's universal and everlasting vision, we can strive to realize the Beloved Community in the body politic.

Jesus' mission statement, the heart of this text and progressive Christian spirituality, centered around the good news of Shalom, wholeness that joins the personal and political and individual abundance and planetary healing. Jesus saw his mission as the incarnation of the prophetic hope articulated by Isaiah:

> *The Spirit of the Lord is upon me,*
>   *because he has anointed me*
>   *to bring good news to the poor.*
> *He has sent me to proclaim release to the captives*
>   *and recovery of sight to the blind,*

to set free those who are oppressed,
to proclaim the year of the Lord's favor. (Luke 4:18-19)

I will repeat Jesus mission statement throughout this book as a clarion call for us to embrace a holistic theology that joins head, heart, and hands, and prayer and protest as central to our mission today. Jesus knew that personal and political healing are interdependent. We experience healing one moment at a time in personal transformation and in healthy relationships. We also promote personal healing through healthy economic and political systems that bring good news to the poor, free the oppressed, and realize our noblest dreams for the historical process. While Jesus did not have political power in any institutional sense and saw politics as serving rather than driving the realization of God's realm, he clearly knew that abundant life required healthy and welcoming communities and a just political order.

Recently, in a Bible Study on the Lord's, or Our Savior's, Prayer, sponsored by my home congregation, Westmoreland Congregational United Church of Christ in Bethesda, Maryland, I asked the participants to describe their vision of the realm of God. Their responses reflected the political and planetary nature of God's realm.

» The lion and the lamb lying down together.
» Justice for everyone.
» A healed planet.
» Humankind and nature are living in harmony.
» A place at the table for everyone.
» The Peaceable Kingdom.
» Seeing God in everyone.

Notice that my companions' responses all involved the vision of a healed world, and a world order quite different from the images of patriarchal, white nationalist, anthropocentric, anti-democratic, and climate change denial put forward by many of our conservative Christian companions. The realm of God embraces all of us, from progressives to populists, descendants of the Mayflower to families crossing the USA border and the great-great grandchildren of slaves and their children and First American victims of genocide. Going beyond zero sum (I win, you lose. You win, I lose.) and scarcity and fear oriented approaches to life, the realm of God seeks abundance for everyone and believes that when one person or group authentically gains, we all gain. The ninety-nine sheep in the fold cannot be safe until the hundredth returns home. In such a healthy community, there is, Mahatma Gandhi asserted, "enough for everyone's need but not everyone's greed." In the spirit of Mary of Nazareth's Magnificat, the sacrifices of the wealthy and privileged enrich the lives of the vulnerable and marginalized, create a healthier society, and save the souls of privileged persons who choose put God ahead of power, prosperity, and place in society. (Luke 1:46-55)

Without a vision of a healed world, we are bound to perish. While we may not make it to the promised land, as Martin Luther King noted in his final address, we must strive one act at a time to promote the moral and spiritual arcs of history. Hope demands the vision of an open future in which our actions make a difference for ourselves, our neighbors, and the planet. The realm, or kindom, of God is not the result of an escapist Second Coming constantly updated but a Millisecond Coming and our moment-by-moment response to God's vision of wholeness embodied on earth as it is in heaven. This must occur in the lives of both persons and communities, and nations and the planet.

Healing the Person, Healing the Planet

Years ago, I first encountered Kenneth Pelletier's *Healthy People in Unhealthy Places,* in which the physician reflected on the importance of healthy work places as essential for overall personal well-being. Pelletier asserted that toxic workplaces harm our bodies as well as our souls. Constant stress and conflict, along with environmental hazards and unpleasant working conditions, weaken the immune system and make persons more susceptible to illness. According to Pelletier, health is environmental as well as a matter of genes and lifestyle. The quality of our workplace, relationships, economic condition, and physical environment can heal or harm, or cure or kill. The quality of our neighborhoods and schools can also cure or kill.

Today, we must add the quality of our national and planetary politics as a factor in overall wellbeing. We cannot separate personal health from public health. While this is obvious in terms of different overall health outcomes based on race and economics, it is becoming apparent that the divisive political atmosphere has put the overall health of the nation at risk as well as the health of our citizens, who face a constant barrage of fearful messages from politicians and the media and witness acts of violence in schools and aimed at minorities and political opponents. Fear is a dominant political emotion. Fear of losing our privilege, prosperity, and power. Fear of others, especially immigrants and persons of color, getting ahead of us. Despite economic progress in the wake of the pandemic, a majority of Americans are pessimistic about the future. Deep down, even the MAGA hatted Trump supporter, knows that the emperor has no clothes, that the days of American unilateral global dominance are numbered, that fake news destroys the soul as well as civil order, and that the planet is in crisis in terms of climate change, immigration, and political upheaval. That is why they shout so loud! Deep down, we know that the enemy is as much within our nation as from the activities of our nation's "enemies." In the words of Walt Kelly's "Pogo" comic strip, posted during the Vietnam War, "we have met the enemy and the enemy is us." Even privileged people feel caught up in the machinations of institutional chaos, believing that they are unable to effect change by their individual efforts. We are under great stress, exacerbated by the victim and grievance mentality of the religious and political right and perpetuated by their political saviors. Deep down, we progressive Christians know that our calling is not only to experience God's transformational love but bring that healing love, with humility and kinship, to our fearful, confused, and mesmerized conservative Christian kin. We are to be their "angels," repeating the biblical counsel given to Mary, Joseph, and the shepherds that first Christmas, and throughout the scriptures "Be not afraid. I am with you."

The book of Revelation speaks of the spirit, enlivening or depressing, churches and institutions and it is clear that our national spirit is sick. No amount of book banning, laws against drag queens, silencing of political opponents, and shouting "Merry Christmas," can restore our nation to health unless the nation's spirit is healed. Yet, health is what we seek even when we follow prevaricating politicians, who offer nothing but ideology, or believe that safety is found in gated communities and automatic weapons.

We need healing and so does our nation and planet. We cannot wait for a constantly updated "rescue operation" from heaven or a politician who promises to be our "retribution" and "make America great again." We must pray for a new national vision, open to new images of what our nation can become, and then become the agents in companionship with God and our fellow citizens in the healing of the spirit of the nation and the life of the planet.

Do You Want to Be Healed? Do You Want to Be a Healer?

John 5:1-15 tells the story of a man who had experienced paralysis for thirty-eight years. He spent his days beside the healing pool, unable to get up because he had no companions to assist him. When Jesus encounters him, Jesus asks a pointed, and seemingly unnecessary question, "Do you want to be made well?" Who doesn't want to experience healing, after all?

To Jesus' surprise, I suspect, the man initially does not say "yes" but gives an accurate but obtuse answer, "I have no one to put me into the pool when the water is stirred up, and while I am making my way someone else steps down ahead of me." He has surrendered his agency, blaming others for his misfortune and believing there is nothing he can do to alter his situation. Disregarding his response, Jesus forces him to make a decision, "Stand up, take your mat and walk." He could have remained paralyzed, but in that moment, he imagines himself walking. He takes a chance. He could fall flat on his face, but he embraces an impossible possibility, stands up, and experiences a cure. The man's commitment to change spiritually was mirrored in a physical change.

Change is difficult for individuals and institutions. Later that day, as the man is walking along, carrying his mat, the religious authorities accost him, reminding him that it is the Sabbath and carrying a mat is a violation of the religious regulations. For a moment, the man forgets his agency and places the entire responsibility on Jesus: "The man who made me well said to me, 'Take up your mat and walk.'"

Jesus observes the interaction, calls the man aside, and gives him a lesson in faith and agency: "See, you have been made well! Do not sin anymore, so that nothing worse happens to you."

At first glance, Jesus' words appear harsh and threatening, and have misled many preachers and readers to identify sin and sickness in a linear fashion. But, that's not the point of the interchange! Jesus is telling the man to claim his agency. Jesus is challenging his passivity: "Don't credit or blame me for your condition. You chose to stand up. You chose to be cured. If you become passive, you will fall into the ways that lead to your paralysis. Accept your role in health and healing. You must claim your healing every day, deepening your agency as well as relationship with the divine healer. Health and healing must be claimed one moment and act at a time. You are my healing companion, and your agency increases my ability to transform your life and the world."

Jesus' question is addressed to us today as we seek to be God's companions in healing the soul of the nation. "Do you want to be healed? Do you want to share in my vision of healing the world?" And, conversely, "Do you want to go on as you have, putting the nation or planet at risk? Do you want to a passive bystander as our nation and the planet descend into chaos and destruction?" Jesus may also address progressive congregations, "Do you want your church to come alive? Do you want the Spirit to arise in your congregation, and fill you with energy and send you out into the street as witnesses of God's Realm? Do you want your congregation and yourself to be agents of destiny and companions in healing the nation and planet?" The choice is yours! Health or illness, life or death, for yourself and our nation.

Recently, I participated in a conference sponsored by the Center for Christogenesis, under the direction of its founder, theologian Ilia Delio. One of the presenters noted that the one of tragedies of the COVID pandemic was that it divided rather than united us and that for many the goal was to get back to normal rather than embracing a new vision of reality, our national life, human relationships, and the relationships of nations. "Getting back to normal" means continuing injustice, disenfranchisement, marginalization, and eventually planetary death. We need a new vision, a new and constantly evolving normal, which embraces and empowers all of us.

The pandemic revealed that economic, political, and environmental borders are an illusion: we are one planet and our survival depends on the well-being of our planetary companions. The pandemic also demonstrated our reliance on undocumented workers, who took risks growing and picking the food we ate, worked in warehouses, and took care of our elders. The same divisive reality, mostly promoted by conservative Christians and the MAGA community, is at work in our responses to climate change and the terrorist insurrection of January 6, 2021. Rather than embracing the "united" states and seeing ourselves connected with one another as American citizens and citizens of the world, we have become more polarized, more divided, and, in the case of white Christian nationalism and conservative Christian politics, more isolated in relationship to pluralism, diversity, and our planetary interdependence. Reasonable health standards, mask wearing, and vaccines became the stuff of protests and conspiracy theories, many of which were promoted by conservative Christians who claimed religious persecution for any limitation of public assembly, forgetting that all rights, even the right to worship, are intimately connected with our responsibility to care for the overall health of others.

We need relational healing. The nature of life is relationship for both persons and communities. We are connected and yet we want to build walls and create divisions that put our lives, future generations, our nation, and the planet at risk.

Do we want to be healed? Do we want to be national and planetary healers? Do we want democracy to flourish in the United States? Do we want our congregations to be healed and to become healed healers in our communities and the nation? If we say "yes," then we will be immediately faced with challenges, internal and external, spiritual and physical, theological and practical. Our agency requires a Beloved Community of companions, allies, and prophets. On our own, we can't respond to every aspect of our national and planetary brokenness. We can't do it alone, nor can we find our healing vocation alone. While we must think globally and look beyond our self-interest, we must start where we are and through our commitment to healing of our nation and planet, join the local and global. If we say "yes," we will need to embark on a journey joining study, practice, and companionship with others committed to national and planetary healing. It will take time to learn the issues, practical responses, the levers of power, and network with people with common healing goals.

Saying "yes" to whole person and whole nation healing will also take sacrifice of time, talent, and treasure. It may mean choosing a simpler lifestyle, reducing your consumption of fossil fuels, lowering your heat in the winter and raising your thermostat in summer. It may mean breaking the cycle of consumption and making a commitment to using fair trade, eco-friendly, and justly produced goods. Saying "yes" to the planet and its vulnerable people means saying "no" to waste, over indulgence, immediate gratification, and private ownership of goods that can be shared such as lawn mowers, tools, and – even! – washing machines and dryers! It means changing our buying and eating habits and becoming an informed, eco-friendly and justice-fair trade consumer. We can have fun without unhealthy consumption: hiking and sports, reading, family gatherings, eating locally sourced, organic food, music, theatre, dance, streaming films, sharing memories, gazing at the stars, playing sports, and holding each other's hands. Processes that enliven and inspire not just products that imprison and impair are called for in response to climate change and economic injustice.

We can't be armchair healers. We can't leave our national healing to others, but must do our part, however insignificant it may seem. Saying "yes" to national and planetary healing means political involvement appropriate to our personality, season of life, and gifts, and moving over to let underrepresented people take the lead in areas dominated by white males and, to a lesser extent, white females.

Healthy Activism

An adage used by physicians and patients is "sometimes the cure is worse than the disease." In a similar fashion, the rock group The Who noted, "Meet the new boss, the same as the old boss" as if to say that revolutions intended to change things for the better often enshrine the same authoritarian policies as their predecessors. One need only to look at China, North Korea, Russia, or Venezuela to see that populist revolutions easily morph into repressive dictatorships. We can tragically look at our own history in which the Great Experiment of democracy failed to include women, indigenous peoples, and slaves. Despite the inclusive language of the USA Constitution, we know that the Founders' vision of equality was limited: only certain people were created equal and possessed God-given rights in the democratic process and law. Women, slaves, and First Americans were disenfranchised legally and politically. Today, those who shout most loudly about Constitutional rights in the United States seem most hellbent to restrict the rights of those who are different than themselves or who oppose their policies, whether in terms of voting or marriage equality.

A truly progressive faith-based political vision must be spiritually grounded. I am not just talking about spiritual practices that reduce our stress and promote health for the long haul of seeking justice in a contentious time. I am also noting the connection between spiritual depth and the willingness to see the holiness in all people, most especially our "enemies." Jesus counseled his followers to "love your enemies and pray for those who persecute you so that you may be children of your Father in heaven, for he makes his sun rise on the evil and on the good and sends rain on the righteous and on the unrighteous." (Matthew 5:43-45)

Jesus' counsel is often seen as impractical in the political realm of compromise and conflict. Indeed, the hard-hearted pragmatism of the religious Christian right exalts the "deadly sins" of incivility, getting even, punishing foes, demonizing immigrants, and retribution over the ethics of compassionate community mandated by Jesus' Sermon on the Mount.

Politics implicitly involves elements of coercion whether in terms of preserving social order, protecting the innocent and the environment, restraining violence, and ensuring national security. Still, we must strive to promote the Peaceable Kingdom even when the realities of civil life compel us, in Whitehead's words, to seek "the best for that impasse." The best may not always be good in the sense of completely eliminating violence or coercion. Even here, in the midst of conflict and challenge, we must cultivate a spirituality of inclusion, healing, reparation, and redemption. The grace we have received and the peace we have experienced motivates us to be agents of grace and peace in the political and foreign policy realms.

Governments may appropriately use coercion at times, but in the spirit of the Prayer of St. Francis, our leaders should be guided by the prayer, "Lord, make me an instrument of peace" and the counsel of the Hippocratic Oath, "do no harm," or as little harm as possible in enforcing laws and protecting borders. While not easily attained, the principles of non-violent civil disobedience employed by Mahatma Gandhi and Martin Luther King can be ideals to guide the use of political power. The "prophetic healing" that I will describe later in this text places our political involvement in the context of our experience of God in our lives, our cultivation of spiritual practices, our vision of God's presence in others and often in their most contentious disguises, and our commitment to seek healing for our relationships in the political and foreign policy realm. We need to be, as Jesus ministry suggests, both tough minded and tender hearted in the performance of political decision making, national security, and justice seeking. Such attitudes only emerge when we – and our leaders – see beyond the pursuit of self-interest and power to the promotion of unity and the interdependence of all life and the spiritual identity of every creature.

In my own life, when I found myself profoundly alienated from Donald Trump, I knew I had to pray for his wellbeing even as I ratcheted up my opposition to his policies and Messianic narcissism. I must pray for his spiritual healing, leaving the result open-ended, even as I am appalled by his self-interested, destructive narcissism and its impact on our nation and his manipulation of conservative Christians who seem more than willing to be manipulated. I still must pray for him: for his healing of mind, body, and spirit. Although I believe that much of conservative Christianity has traded Jesus' way of love for ruthless power, I must also see the divine in my fellow Christians as I pray that they have their own "come to Jesus" moment just as I have to be open to my own "come to Jesus" moments. If God's grace embraces me, then it must embrace those I assume are most diabolical in their politics and use of power. To turn the evangelical phrase on its head, "hate the sin, and love the sinner," we must seek to love the Trumps of the world and their conservative Christian minions while doing our best to nullify their power and policies.

In an interdependent universe, there is no "other." We are all entangled and will ultimately flourish of fail together. We need the MAGA supporters and they need us. As Martin Luther King affirmed:

> It all boils down to this, that all life is interrelated. We are caught in an inescapable network of mutuality, tied into a single garment of destiny. Whatever affects one directly, affects all indirectly. We are made to live together because of the interrelated structure of reality.[7]

No nation, no community, no species, no race, no individual can go it alone. We need one another to flourish as nations and persons: "For some strange reason I cannot be what I ought to be until you are what you ought to be. And you can never be what you ought to be until I am what I ought to me. That's the way the God's universe is made."[8]

Affirming the unity of life takes vision, spiritual maturity, and the trust that there is "something of God" in those we oppose and that divine identify joins us not only in the wondrous diversity of life but also in the contentiousness of politics. Our own healing and salvation are connected to their healing and salvation, and wholeness requires us to commit to healing the body politic in all its divisive dysfunctionality. The Beloved Kingdom utilizes power but aims at healing and reconciliation in our hearts, relationships, and political policies.

Nurturing a Robust and Activist Progressive Spirit

Healing involves body, mind, spirit, and relationships. Jesus' ministry enjoins us to be both heavenly minded, concerned for

---

7   Martin Luther King, *Testament of Hope* (New York: Harper One, 2023), 254.
8   Martin Luther King, *A Knock at Midnight* (New York: Warner Books), 208.

the eternal and infinite, and also earthly good, entangled in the healing of institutions, communities, nations, and the planet.

Living with Jesus the Healer. Jesus the healer is alive in our time. The healing ministry of Jesus embraces the personal and social and sets people free from socially imposed as well as self-imposed limitations.

In this practice, follow in the spirit of Holy Reading or Lectio Divina, focusing on the personal and social dimensions of divine healing as you read the following scripture:

> *Now there was a woman who had been suffering from a flow of blood for twelve years. She had endured much under many physicians and had spent all that she had, and she was no better but rather grew worse. She had heard about Jesus and came up behind him in the crowd and touched his cloak, for she said, "If I but touch his cloak, I will be made well." Immediately her flow of blood stopped, and she felt in her body that she was healed of her disease. Immediately aware that power had gone forth from him, Jesus turned about in the crowd and said, "Who touched my cloak?" And his disciples said to him, "You see the crowd pressing in on you; how can you say, 'Who touched me?'" He looked all around to see who had done it. But the woman, knowing what had happened to her, came in fear and trembling, fell down before him, and told him the whole truth. He said to her, "Daughter, your faith has made you well; go in peace, and be healed of your disease." (Mark 5:25-34)*

1) Begin with a time of silence and prayerful openness to God.
2) Read the scripture twice, pausing between each reading and following the second reading.
3) Listen for a word or image that comes to you in the course of your meditation.
4) Consider the word or image that comes to you, asking for its meaning in your life.
5) Ask God how this inspiration might relate to your life-

style, relationships, or citizenship and political involvement.

6) Give thanks for God's inspiration in your life and pray
to embody God's guidance in your personal life and citizenship.

7) Look for insights related to your experience throughout
the day and as you watch the news or read news feeds or
the newspaper.

8) When insights occur, ask for God's guidance in terms
of living out your faith in your relationships and in the
public sphere.

Holy reading awakens us to God's "still, small voice" whether
in your personal life or citizenship, alerting us to the reality that
the world is saved one moment and action at a time.

Finding Your Healing Path Social transformation requires patience, wisdom, hospitality, and a cosmopolitan spirit. Prophetic
ministry joins the prophet's encounter with the Holy and social
involvement. We must challenge injustice and incivility with an
alternative vision of our nation and political action, rooted in the
wisdom of Jesus's Sermon on the Mount, Luke 4:18-19, and Matthew 25:34-40 and the prophetic protesters of Israel. Challenge
and critique often devolve into hatred and alienation apart from a
commitment to spiritual practices which take us from party spirit to global healing. Moreover, the stresses of religious and social
transformation can undermine our physical, spiritual, and relational health. We can be healthy champions of justice through
regular commitments to prayer and meditation.

In this section, I invite you to explore a simple prayer practice, involving focusing on your breath.

Sitting comfortably, begin breathing slowly and deeply. Feel
each breath filling your body with energy and calm. Feel each
breath bringing peace and releasing stress. Experience yourself
centered in Christ's Spirit, and sharing this Spirit with all cre-

ation, including those whom we challenge. In this simple practice
I learned from contemplative activist Allan Armstrong Hunter:

1) Breathe deeply, focusing on the words "I breathe God's
   Spirit deeply in."
2) Let your breath fill your whole being.
3) Exhale, focusing on the words, "I breathe God's Spirit out again." (Knowing your breath adds peace to the
   world.)
4) Let your inhaling and exhaling connect you with friend
   and foe alike, and with the human and non-human
   worlds.

You may choose to follow this practice whenever you find
yourself anxious about a personal situation, relationship, or a political or planetary situation. As you feel stress or anxiety, pause
amid your tasks, and take a few centering breaths, filling your spirit with God's Spirit. From practicing this breath prayer, you may
discover that we are all connected in the Spirit. We share the same
breath, require the same nurture, and find wholeness when we see
each other as God's beloved children and kin.

THEOLOGICAL HEALING FOR OURSELVES, OUR NATION, AND THE PLANET

For some time now the principle interest of my life is no longer Fossil Man, but the Man of Tomorrow; or, more exactly, the "God of tomorrow," since I am more and more convinced that the great event of our time is a kind of change in the face of God.[9]

The world must have a God; but our concept of God must be extended as the dimensions of our world are extended.[10]

Theology matters. The emergence of a lively progressive Christian theology matters. Our beliefs shape our character and political involvements. A changed vision of God leads to changes in ethics, politics, and relationships. Today, conservative Christi-

---

9   "Letter to Idea Treat," August 30, 1950. Quoted in Ursula King, *Spirit of Fire: The Life and Vision of Teilhard de Chardin* (Maryknoll, NY: Orbis Books, 2015), 204.

10   Pierre Teilhard de Chardin, "Letters from a Traveler." Quoted in Ursula King, *Spirit Fire: The Life and Vision of Teilhard de Chardin* (Maryknoll, NY: Orbis Books, 2015), 58.

anity needs a changed god, just as we progressives need fully to claim and experience a personal relationship with the divinity we can believe in. Our vision of God can shape the politics of climate change, inclusiveness, immigration, economics, diversity, the relationship of church and state, and even our attitudes about vaccines and masks.

The authoritarian and coercive vision of God, prized by conservative Christians, leads to a religious life that demands absolute obedience and divides the world in terms of friend and foe. The authoritarian and monarchical God, ruling on high and threatening his opponents with eternal damnation, appoints representatives who rule, or claim to rule, by "divine right" and Christian, Muslim, or Hindu "dominion." From this perspective, pluralism is a threat and must be marginalized, punished, or eliminated. To give credence to contrasting positions threatens our own sense of truth and power. For example, in the area of biblical authority, if Genesis creation story is proven to be poetry and scientifically inaccurate, the divinity, cross, and resurrection must be called into question. American followers of the authoritarian God must adhere to the fundamentals of faith, clearly revealed in scripture, despite the fact that conservative Christians tend to privilege American capitalism and individualism rather than the clearly stated biblical vision of prophetic communalism, economic equity, and social justice. The words of the prophets, Mary's Magnificat, and Jesus' Sermon on the Mount have no place in their political policies.

Followers of absolutist and authoritarian world views claim to know the truth in its fullness, despite the curious fact that conservative Christians tend not only to be science deniers but also election deniers and turn a blind eye to the thousands of lies perpetrated by their chosen American messiah, proving themselves ironically to be the most unrepentant relativists. The quest for political and religious absolutism puts at risk democracy, diversity, and voting rights, whether in 1930's Germany and its emerging Reich Church or 2020's USA and its idolatrous Trump Church.

We need to present a lively, believable, and earth transformative alternative to the visions of a small spirited and vindictive god that inspires small and mean-spirited politics which see truth and value as limited to one way and condemn theological and political outsiders as agents of evil and unworthy of ethical consideration. A brittle god who requires absolute obedience leads to a brittle authoritarian religion and politics. Indeed, faith in the transactional God is transactional in nature. If you accept God's way, you will be blessed with eternal life. If you question the one truth faith and politics, you are threatened with damnation. There is just one, clearly demarcated way to salvation, and all other paths lead to eternal punishment. This same absolute loyalty is demanded by God's self-appointed religious and political representatives. To go against God's appointed messenger is to be seen as unpatriotic, Marxist, and a nation-hater. Such a God demands sacrifice: in this case, sacrifice of our intellect and creativity, and also the sacrifice of that God's enemies. Such a god, however, is too small for a universe of a trillion galaxies and a planet of diverse cultures, religions, and ethnicities. Such a god is backward looking, fixated on past sins and promoting yesterday's science, ethics, and doctrine.

In contrast to cramped and binary images of God, cosmopolitan, inclusive, and dynamic visions of God, embracing diversity, lead to large spirited and welcoming politics. The God of Tomorrow delights in a trillion-galaxy universe, the big bang and evolving planets, and human and non-human diversity.

I believe that the Living God is all-embracing and encourages us to grow in wisdom and stature and in embrace of reality in its wondrous diversity. The Loving and Living God inspires loving politics and counsels loving our enemies, even as we challenge their political policies. In the words of James Baldwin, "If the concept of God has any viability or use, it can only make us larger, freer, and more loving. If God cannot do this, then it's time to get rid of Him."[11]

11   James Baldwin, *The Fire Next Time* (New York: Vintage Books, 1992), 61.

A World Transforming Vision of God

Theology matters – and humble-spirited progressive Christian theology matters - and we must not let conservative Christianity define the theological and biblical playing field. We too are Christians, and our beliefs can change the world in life-affirming and healing ways. We are as faithful and committed as those who claim to hold the keys to God's kingdom and the secret of salvation and scripture. We need not take second chair in sharing God's good news or God's vision of inclusion, salvation, and scripture. Progressive Christians must boldly, yet humbly, proclaim an alternative theological vision that reflects and supports the insights of science, religious, cultural, and ethnic diversity, and joins spiritual values with political action in a pluralistic society. While humble in spirit and pluralistic in approach to the perspectives of other religious traditions, including other Christian perspectives, we must not surrender the faith we affirm and the ethics and politics that flow from our vision of a relational, earth-affirming God. In sharing our faith as progressives, we may find ourselves healing the spirits of nones, dones, and those who have abandoned conservative Christianity in quest to experience the good news of Jesus.

The God we need for today and tomorrow in the quest to save the soul of the nation and planet must be large enough to embrace the universe, our diverse planet and its religious pluralism, and challenges to our planetary survival. With gratitude to the theological framers of the past, we need to discover a God – or a vision of God – and a vision of scripture that can take us to infinity and beyond! A Relational and Innovative God invites us to expect great things of ourselves and Godself as we seek to heal the world. A Forward-Looking God invites us to be companions in healing and building the world and become God's agents bringing wholeness to God's experience of the world.

In a world of constant change and ever-expanding diversity, we must be willing to experience God as the ultimate Change Agent. We must be willing to affirm that the face of God we see is also constantly changing to respond to the uniqueness of this moment and our current situation and that shapes our theology and spirituality. We need to open our senses and intellect to greater images of God. We need a big-spirited, cosmic and cosmopolitan God, and as Charles Hartshorne says, a self-surpassing and evolving God, who is also as near as our next breath and for whom our day-to-day struggles as persons and responsible residents of a planet in crisis matter. God's best years are ahead, and so are ours as we seek to embody a more vital church and more perfect union.

Practical Theology as Life-Changing Theology

Theology is not an arm chair discipline for me, nor should it be for you. Theology is a matter of spiritual and planetary and national survival. It is a matter of peoples' bodies and souls, as well as their minds. These days I am more convinced than ever of the lively interdependence and importance of theology, ministry, and spirituality. As I claimed earlier, I believe that the survival of progressive Christianity, including our fallible and sometimes dispirited congregations, is essential to the survival of the planet and our nation. Despite the fallibility of our churches and our, at times, lukewarm spirituality and worship, I believe that progressive Christianity is necessary as a positive force for personal and planetary transformation, a creative counterforce and alternative vision to the intentional destruction of the planet and intolerance of otherness practiced by conservative politicians and their spiritual leaders, and as a firewall to blunt the impact of the Christian nationalism and idolatry that has become viral in conservative Christianity, and that is often seen as the only representation of Christianity by seekers, exiles from the church, and the news media.

Today, the primary theological question for me, as it was for First/Old Testament scholar Terry Fretheim, is not "Does God exist?" but "What kind of God do you believe in? What kind of God inspires your values, relationships, and politics?" Will God be the sanction of the status quo and primary proponent of white nationalism and binary politics or will God be the prime mover in the creation of a healthy planet, united in the quest for justice, global partnership, and healthy diversity.

To reiterate, we need a God big enough to embrace the radical changes in science, technology, communication, globalism, and climate change, we face now and will face in the future. We need a God who embraces and welcomes pluralism, promotes creativity and adventure, and encourages new visions of human possibility. God is not locked into an ideal golden age whether it be a mythical Garden of Eden, the first century church, the theocratic Holy Roman Empire, or the ambiguous world of our "Christian founders" or the white, male dominated world of the 1950s. We need to embrace an agile and innovative God whose creativity matches and goes beyond our own creativity, and whose adventurous spirit inspires our own adventures. While we cannot claim to fully know this God, or assume that we can fully fathom God's will, we are compelled in light of authoritarian, binary, violent, and destructive images of God, to humbly image a lively and inclusive God, whose presence embraces the universe and whose love encompasses the cells of our bodies and the souls of octopuses. We are compelled to be both spiritually bold and politically humble as we seek God's realm "on earth as it is in heaven."

Holistic Activism

Progressive Christians' activism needs to be grounded in the interplay of theology, spirituality, scripture, science, and the wisdom of other faiths and the surrounding culture. If we believe that God is omnipresent and omni-active, in contrast to the all determining and divisive deity, then we must affirm that divine revelation is broadcast generously and globally. The heavens declare the glory of God and so do the wisdom givers of every culture and religious tradition. God's presence guides even those whom we challenge politically and socially. Beneath what we perceive as their errant and dangerous theologies, God is at work. Adherents of small-spirited theologies are also seeking wholeness, albeit in ways we believe to be dangerous to our nation and the planet. We cannot hate them because, despite appearances, there is "something of God" in them!

Scripture as a Witness to Creative Transformation and Pluralistic Witness

Conservative Christians claim to be the purveyors of biblical truth. They describe themselves as Bible-believing and condemn others, such as progressive Christians, as relativists who have forsaken the clear meaning of scripture in our affirmation of pluralism, human rights, science, LGBTQ+ persons, and earth care. The conservative mantra has been "the Bible says it, I believe it, and that settles it" even though conservatives fixate on a few passages related to homosexuality and demonize drag queens, despite no biblical prohibitions for its practice, and de-emphasize or ignore the hundreds of verses championing social justice, the reallocation of resources, the embrace of strangers and immigrants, and the socialist economics of the early church. The Second Amendment and marriage of God and gun ownership – "God, guns, and Trump" - has supplanted Jesus' affirmation, "blessed are the peacemakers" and "love your enemies." Embracing false political narratives, prevaricating politicians, and conspiracy theories has become the norm of conservative Christians political perspective despite the biblical admonition not to bear false witness. Once ardent critics of those who asserted that "the end justifies the means," conservative Christians in politics now justify any means necessary to preserve Christian superiority and political control, including subverting democracy and limiting voting rights to people who look like them. Honoring their deliverer, referred to jokingly – or was it? – as "Orange Jesus," and his upside-down Bible and armed with the mantra, "the Bible tells me so," conservative Christianity fosters a crusade mentality against any opposing viewpoint, which must be defeated at any cost.

We cannot let conservative Christians own scripture any more than we can allow them to own patriotism, ethics, and prayer. In fact, we need to be God's companions in healing the spirit of scripture, which has been broken and rendered dangerous by its use as justification for hatred, incivility, injustice, xenophobia, racism, and homophobia. In response to authoritarian theology, politics, and visions of God, progressive Christians can present an alternative vision of scripture, a living bible and loving bible, historically grounded, open to creative transformation, and adaptable to a changing world. We can reclaim the vision of a living, evolving, liberating scripture, whose message is grounded in love, justice, hospitality, and Shalom. We don't need the fiction of an "inerrant" scripture. We need an inspiring and enlivening, relevant and contextual scripture emerging from the dance of Divinity and our spiritual parents in bygone days and still being written today in our own spiritual adventures and quest for Shalom.

The Blessings of Lamentations

While there are many scriptural lenses with which to view God's presence in the world, I have chosen Lamentations 3:22-24 to illuminate a progressive vision of God's relationship to the world and, accordingly, scripture and political involvement.

> *The steadfast love of God never ceases,*
> *his mercies never come to an end;*
> *they are new every morning;*
> *great is your faithfulness.*
> *"The LORD is my portion," says my soul,*
> *"therefore I will hope in God."*

Lamentations 3:22-24 presents a novel vision of scripture to go with the novel face of Tomorrow's God. We need a scripture of tomorrow as well as yesterday. A scripture embedded in history and agile enough to change as the world changes. Perhaps traditional theology's understanding of the nature and scope of revelation went astray due to its reading of scripture and constructing its vision of God with greater attention to the children of Aristotle and Aquinas than the mystics and prophets of the Bible. In following Aristotle's world view and its privileging of an unchanging, unfeeling, and uninvolved god, and a one-sided world-denying and inaccurate reading of Plato, traditional theology fixated on the eternal, unchanging, static aspects of reality and promoted a backward-looking spirituality of ascent and escape rather than embeddedness and incarnation. History aimed toward escaping from destruction rather than the Peaceable Realm.

Traditional theology proclaimed a changeless God, who cannot grow or know anything new, or innovate in the course of history beyond God's original vision, and who is complete in Godself. Traditional theology privileged a static, dogmatic, and backward looking, theology and interpretation of revelation, sure of its answers, scorning questions, and absolutizing its channels of authority, whether they be scripture to be read literally in only one way; ecclesiastical leadership whose power and manifest destiny could not be questioned, even when it strayed from the way of Jesus and the prophets with Crusades, Inquisitions, and the Doctrine of Discovery; and sacraments whose possession was restricted to male church authorities, human institutions, and supernatural formulae, disenfranchising women, persons other faiths, and indigenous people, whether Celtic or First American.

In promoting the vision of a changeless and authoritarian-unilateral acting God and static understandings of scripture and revelation, traditional theology traded the living God for a lifeless doctrine, a personal relationship with Jesus for a set of rules, and a dynamic and evolving scriptural witness for authoritarian irrelevance and inquisition. The love of God was eclipsed by the love of power, and the need to control the faithful and also control God, who is the great iconoclast and source of novelty. The Galilean image of God in Jesus was supplanted, as Whitehead says, by Caesar and his minions, the body of Christ morphed into Empire, Reich Church and now Trump Church. The Grand Inquisitor and his ecclesiastical morality police won the day, and the earthy and intimate, welcoming and unbounded, Jesus of the Gospels was eclipsed by abstractions, theological and ecclesiastical boundaries, power plays, and theological threats.

In contrast to those who would deaden and freeze the Living and Loving Word of God to literal words, the God of scripture is lively and alive, relational and personal, changed and changing, sometimes inconsistent and troubling, and dare we say evolving and inspiring evolution. This is the God of Tomorrow who embraces and transforms the past and inspires the present. A god of history, hope, and transformation, that places on equal footing the marriage of change and changelessness and trusts evolving wisdom amid the maelstrom of uncertainty. God is involved in history and God wants us to be as well. Just wages and equal access matters to God and it should matter to us.

While the author of Lamentations was unaware of contemporary cosmology, evolutionary processes, and the heliocentric world, it is clear that the author's words describe a world and deity that is new every morning and speaks to our expanding visions of God, spirituality, and the human adventure. Accordingly, we must read them poetically and spiritually, dynamically and inclusively, as fingers pointing to the moon and not the wholeness of divinity. We must also read them – and the scriptural witness in its entirety - with knowledge that God is the reality in whom we live and move and have our being, and also that the God in whom we have our becoming and is thus present and active in all creation. Revelation is ubiquitous and evolving, not confined to sacrament, institution, or scripture. Nor is revelation restricted to a particular religion, political affiliation, or ethnic group.

God is on the move and so should our religions and politics. Listen once more to the witness of Lamentation 3: *The steadfast love of the LORD never ceases, God's mercies never come to an end.* In a time of personal and national crisis, the sixth century BCE author of Lamentations is sustained by the interplay of steadfastness and infinity, of transcendence and intimacy. God's love never ceases, God's mercies have no boundary, no exclusion in time or space. Centuries ago, Bonaventure and Nicholas of Cusa proclaimed the intimate infinity of God with the words:

» God is a circle (or infinite sphere)
» Whose center is everywhere
» And whose circumference is nowhere.

These words aptly describe the God of Lamentations 3 and I believe the God of Tomorrow. These words challenge us to a politics of affirmation and inclusion. God centers everyone, and includes all creation, inspiring us to promote reverence for life in all its amazing and contrasting diversity. Reverence for life means that we promote the wellbeing of those who differ from us, and the full spectrum of the rainbow sexually, spiritually, and ethnically. There is no other, ultimately. We are connected in origin, history, and destiny. *Ubuntu*, "I am because of you. We are because of one another." Universality of value and reverence for life promote political processes that embrace everyone.

Grounded in the vision of an all-embracing and evolving God, I approach Lamentations, and the scriptural witness, as a dynamic and open-spirited series of affirmations congruent with a changing universe, God, scripture, and spirituality. Affirmations that are humble and bold, affirmative and poetic. Flexible, not fixed, and personal and concrete rather than generic and abstract.

Open your heart to friend and stranger alike for *the steadfast love of God never ceases*. The steadfast love of God is no abstraction. It touches our hearts, transforms our spirits, and makes a way where there is no way. The steadfast love of God embraces everyone, without exception. As Jesus says, the sun shines and the rain falls on the just and unjust alike, and so should our ethical and political consideration.

The Divine One centers all things, is their deepest reality, is ever present and ever faithful in real, passing, evolving time. The words "nothing can separate us from the love of God" (Romans 8:38-39) are both pastoral and theological. God is our protector, companion, and comfort in the face of death, catastrophe, persecution, and illness. God will not let us, or anyone, down. God's intimate love is constant and active in our lives. Ontologically speaking, God is not separate from us, God is within us, as near as our next breath, the energy of love that gives life and vitality to all things, and the prophetic voice who awakens us to the moral and spiritual arcs that flow through us and the universe. If God is joined with us, then we are joined with one another.

God's love births forth creativity and compassion and guides the long journey of evolution and planet making and, today, planetary healing. God is not "other" but is the beyond – the future lure – moving within each moment of experience. Conversely, we are within God, and so is the friend, foe, and stranger, constantly shaping God's experience and inspiring God's action in the world. Intimate connection with God promotes intimate connection with the wondrous variety of human – and non-human – life.

Let us rejoice for *God's mercies never come to an end.* The divine endlessness encompasses space and time as it unfolds. God's love takes us to "infinity and beyond," as Buzz Lightyear of "Toy Story," proclaims. Wherever there is existence, God's mercies are at work. There is no final resting place for God's love reflected in God's inspiration, revelation, and care for stranger and kin. Love makes the world go round and guides the movements of stars and planets. God guides the better angels of our nature, when we are tempted to become agents of alienation. The evolution of our planet and its institutions reflects God's blessing of the marriage of unity and diversity. God's mercies give birth to religious and cultural pluralism and extend far beyond the church and our beloved nation to embrace the whole Earth. Recognizing the merciful reality "in whom we live and move and have our being," (Acts 17:28) and "our becoming," inspires us to see all creatures as words of God, receiving and giving revelation. God's mercies never end temporally: death does not halt God's love nor does our human waywardness.

The ever-expanding circumference of God's love is nowhere, embracing pluralism, frontiers of science, and the ever-receding horizons of human and non-human possibility. God's love expands as the universe expands. God's love contracts to care for the smallest of things. Mercy means relationship, and relationship means change in God and the world. God's mercies are found in the scientist struggling with the moral use of Artificial Intelligence, the protester advocating for full humanity for LGBTQ+ and immigrants on our borders and confronting climate change, and God's mercies are even found in the MAGA hatted worshippers frightened of immigrants and anxious about losing power in a multi-ethnic future. As I noted earlier, there is no "other." We are a human and national family, in which, as a church placard asserts, "all are pilgrims and none are strangers." A God without an outside, a God whose spirit moves through all the cells of this wondrous and tragic universe, is constantly changing, evolving, and growing – not afraid of novelty – and loving creation in its waywardness and tragic beauty.

Stretching out into infinity (and beyond) the planetary and historical process reflects God's revelation, a revelation that is lively and contextual, all-embracing and life-transforming, we can affirm: *God's mercies are new every morning.* God's mercy calls us to future possibilities rather than past achievements. Or as one of my favorite hymns affirms, "Great is thy faithfulness, O dear Creator, Morning by morning new mercies I see. All I have needed thy hand has provided. Great is thy faithfulness God unto me."

God's novelty, God's lively mercies embrace all creation, without exception, even when we turn away. They are endless in time, space, and impact. God is the Ultimate Empath, Most Moved Mover, and Most Understanding Relativist, and also the Inspiration of the Moral and Spiritual Arcs – the arcs of healing and wholeness – moving through the universe and us. God is the ultimate Change Agent, challenging us to ever wider circles of adventure and community. Such ever-expanding novelty inspires a lifestyle and politics of abundance. In God's world, life is abundant and there is always enough to go around, spiritually and economically. The authentic growth and success of others contributes to our own growth and success. Generosity of spirit and resource uplifts everyone and heals the souls of persons and nations.

Embodying new mercies, giving birth to all creation and each moment of experience, the God of Tomorrow, the Infinite and Intimate One, proclaims a universal and ever-expanding spiral of revelation. The heavens shout the glory of God, and so do the cells of our bodies. Babies and parents of all kinds give birth to divine wisdom. In God's evolving world and human adventure, pluralism is not a fall from grace, but the varieties of human religious experience reflect God's bountiful and generous revelation. A merciful God provides many pathways to wholeness for all creation, working within the chance, accident, and decision-making, of history and personal life. The future is not decided in advance but emerges through the partnership of God and creation. This theology will preach, and we should preach it boldly to reclaim our spiritual vitality and vocation to give witness to a progressive faith seekers, disaffected conservative and evangelical Christians, and advocates for justice and earth-care. This theology will not only preach, but it will also reach – seekers, disaffiliated nones, and disaffected evangelicals – with its message of a living, loving, evolving, embracing, healing, and intimate God who is out to heal us and not hurt us and unite and not divide.

The Church as a Laboratory of Prophetic Spirituality

Inspired and inspiring theology leads to spiritual transformation. Trusting God's care and support, we can affirm that *"God is my portion," says my soul, "therefore I will hope in him."* The spirituality and theology of the future, the God and faith of tomorrow, are grounded in feasting on the divine. "Taste and see that God is good," chants the Psalmist (Psalm 34:9). We need congregations that are places of spiritual nurture, communities of prophetic spirit persons who inspire others to join spirituality and political transformation.

Karl Rahner prophesied that the church of the future must be mystic or not exist at all. I agree with Rahner, and believe that the church of the future, the spirituality and theology of the future, and the politics of the future, must image the divine – the nature of reality - in ways that promote and integrate mysticism, healing, and prophetic faith. What the world needs as it moves toward wider horizons of planetary community is an embodied spirituality, a spirituality with skin that sends us into the streets, the Halls of Congress, and the soup kitchen motivated by hope, hope in the faithful and dynamic God, the healing presence of spirit, and the prophetic horizon. Hope inspires us to believe that we can be agents of world healing despite the uncertainties of our future as a nation and planet.

The progressive church must become a laboratory for spiritual transformation, committed to joining the inner and outer journeys of global transformation. To teach meditation and encourage protest. To challenge injustice and imagine new possibilities for reconciliation. To welcome healing prayer and Pentecostal ecstasy and also be open to the prayers of the Earth, the prayers of non-human thin places, and forgotten indigenous peoples. Spirituality must be embodied, historical, and global. While we may choose a particular focus to our spiritual lives – centering prayer, Zen meditation, Ignatian imagination, reiki healing touch, walking prayer, *lectio divina* – the wondrous global spiritual smorgasbord welcomes us to take the portion that speaks to us at a particular time of our soul's journey.

God is moving in our lives and our world. God beckons us to be contemplative activists. God will not give up on us, on the starts and stops of evolution, and the future that lies ahead. We don't know the future nor can we control it, but we can discover a Loving, Intimate, Flexible Companion, big enough for all our adventures, and calling us to be big enough to claim our vocation as God's companions in healing the world.

Progressive Theological Affirmations.

A living scripture and lively theology promote a world-trans-forming faith. Theology, spirituality, scripture, and social activism can't be separated. They inspire and shape one another. Accordingly, progressive Christianity promotes what Rufus Jones describes as "affirmative mysticism." Encountering God inspires us to seek justice and love mercy. While rigid, backward looking, doctrines constrict, lively and open-ended theological affirmations encourage creativity and hospitality. Although we can never fully describe God's presence in the world and our lives, these twelve affirmations can become the content of our message, the framework which describes our world, and the good news we share in our relationships and political involvement. These affirmations will preach, teach, empower, and energize us to transform the earth in "just such a time as this." We can proclaim them with the same boldness, albeit seasoned by humility, as our conservative Christian kin, claiming the theological playing field and theological activism for the merciful God whose love is new every morning and whose compassion embraces the earth in its bountiful diversity.

God is love and God's love embraces everyone. No one is outside the circle of God's love. God seeks to heal all creation and every person. The center is everywhere, enlivening and energizing everyone, and the circumference is nowhere, encompassing everyone. Accordingly, our calling is to love those who see themselves as our enemies, challenging their viewpoints and actions with love and seeking their authentic wholeness. A politics of love can take sides and play political hardball, that is, strongly and non-violently asserting our position and protesting injustice, in the quest to align with the moral and spiritual arcs of history, but even then the goal is reconciliation, healing, and if we must engage in the scrum of politics to minimize harm.

God loves the world and desires this world to reflect God's values. God is embedded in history and the activities of humankind and the non-human world. The world is created by love and each life is birthed by love. Condemned as a heretic because he questioned the theologically problematic, yet orthodox, doctrines of original sin and human depravity, St. Pelagius asserts that every child enters the world bearing the face of God. God's love is empathetic and creative. God shapes the world moment by moment and over the long haul according to God's vision of Shalom. God also experiences the joy and sorrow of the world. Accordingly, we affirm this world and history as important to God and worthy of our concern. What happens in this world matters to God. God needs us to be fully God in our world. In our personal and political lives, are we adding or subtracting from God's experience of beauty and God's quest for Shalom.

God's revelation is global as well as individual. God is present in Christ and also in the diverse religious, scriptures, and cultural paths of humankind. God is constantly inspiring us, calling us to embody God's vision of Shalom and Wholeness in our lives and citizenship. As God's companions, we are writing scriptures right now in partnership with God as we share in God's healing adventure. God's love deep down inspires foe, friend, and stranger, and binds us by a love that never ends. Recognizing the ubiquity of divine inspiration, we look for the wisdom of children and strangers and open to areas of common ground with those who otherwise are our opponents.

Jesus reveals God's vision for our lives and the world. Openness to a relationship with Jesus transforms and heals our lives and relationships. Intimate and infinite in influence, Jesus is the reflection of God's character and purpose in the universe and our lives. Jesus' spiritual energy and loving power provides a path to wholeness for all persons. In embracing Jesus' way, God's energy flows through us, inspiring us to be little Christs and Bodhisattvas. Accordingly, we can expect great things of ourselves as Jesus' representatives in the world and expect great things of God as Jesus' power flows through us to heal and reconcile.

Nothing can separate us from the love of God. There is no circumference to God's love in time, place, and person. All belong to God's circle of love and even when we must challenge the political policies and actions of others, we see them as God's beloved children. No one is lost or forsaken. Separation is an illusion. There is no "other" and when we embrace otherness, even political otherness, the world is renewed and repaired.

You can experience God and have a personal relationship with God in Jesus Christ. The Infinite is the Intimate. God is constantly moving in our unique lives. Moment by moment, God invites us to a relationship filled with possibility, adventure, and love. God is the Great Companion and Jesus is our Sibling and Kin, inviting us to walk in the light of God.

Jesus is our companion and guide who constantly awakens us to God's vision for our lives and the world. A transformed progressive theology awakens us to a transformed relationship with Jesus. Jesus is our companion, our sibling and friend, who "walks with us and talks to us and tells us we are God's own." We can experience Jesus' Spirit in our lives, animating, guiding, and challenging us to full humanity. Following the way and teachings of Jesus our goal is loving transformation even in the middle of conflict-ridden situations.

God seeks the Beloved Community for our personal, communal, national, and planetary relationships. God's aim for the world is a community where everyone belongs and where everyone rejoices in the wellbeing of their neighbor. God invites us beyond self-interest to world loyalty.

God inspires the moral and spiritual arcs of history. God is at work in history and in our lives aiming at the emergence of God's realm in history. God is the source of prophetic unrest and healing compassion in our individual lives and in the lives of communities. History is unfinished and aiming at God's vision of wholeness. Our actions can add to or diminish God's progress in history. To affirm the moral and spiritual arcs of history is not to deny the catastrophic threats that confront us. When I read my newsfeed or watch cable news, I often feel that we are going backward morally and regressing spiritually. Some days I feel that there is little I can do, other than enjoy my life and support my family and friends, in light of the destructive and overwhelming powers of those who intentionally foment violence, destroy the planet, threaten democracy, and stifle human diversity and rights, often in the name of Jesus. When I remember the moral and spiritual arcs quietly moving in the world, I am once again inspired to do something beautiful for God and choose to be a companion in healing the world one act at a time.

All life is interdependent. We are connected. We are one. There is no other and that includes God who is the deepest reality moving through our lives and communities, joining us and all creation. Our wellbeing and the wellbeing of our nation depend on the wellbeing of our planetary companions. Our lives matter and contribute to the health or disease of our communities and the planet.

To exist is to have value: the non-human and human world are valuable. We live in a world of praise in which "creation sings and around us rings the music of the spheres." The non-human world is alive, matters apart from its benefit to us, and deserves our ethical consideration. We should minimize non-human pain and recognize that the non-human world has value of its own apart from our interests. Our calling is to heal God's world in partnership with our human and non-human kin.

History is open-ended for God and us. What we do matters. We are shaping the world by our actions. Our actions shape history. They also shape God's experience. In the words of Mother (Saint) Teresa, our calling is to "do something beautiful for God" through acts of love, reconciliation, and earth healing. Our vocation is to be God's companions in healing the earth. Apart from our efforts, God cannot repair and heal the world. Our actions add to or detract from God's impact in the world and in the future of our nation. With God as our companion, all things are possible in healing this good Earth.

Nurturing a Robust and Activist Progressive Spirit

Vital and world changing theology emerges in relationship to lively and energizing spiritual practices. The great religious traditions arose through the impact of mystical experiences: Moses and the burning bush, Buddha sitting beneath the Bodhi tree, Mohammed in the cave hearing the voice of Allah, Jesus finding his vocation in the wilderness and embracing his mission in the Garden. Open-spirited theology that changes our lives and the world is a gift of grace, the infinite and intimate call of God. God calls and we respond, and our response is enhanced and energized by spiritual practices.

Finding Your Theological Vision. Without a flexible vision, we can become spiritually rudderless. A personal theological vision, grounded in the interplay of tradition, culture, scripture, and spiritual experience, provides a framework for decision-making and political involvement. I describe this interplay as "theo-spirituality." In this exercise, I invite you to go on a theological vision quest.

Over a period of days or weeks, begin this flexible spiritual practice in the spirit of "ask, seek, and knock," praying for a theological vision to energize and guide your life, relationships, and citizenship. Each day, take time for silence, asking for a living theological vision. Recognizing that when we move, our ideas also move, take your vision on a walk. If walking is difficult, imagine yourself on a journey. Let theological visions and questions emerge without judgement. Each day enter these visions in a theological journal. Over a period of time, create a framework of affirmations that you can live by. Always be willing to change your visionary affirmations, if you have new insights, encounters, religious experiences, and vocational wisdom.

There is No Other. A recurring theme of this text is that the essence of life is graceful interdependence. In the intimate relatedness of life, we create one another. Our joys and sorrows are one. There is no other, despite contrasting political viewpoints, cultures, personalities, and the essential diversity of life.

Feelings of unity can emerge through mystical experiences. They also occur as a result of our spiritual affirmations and contemplative practices. Monastic activist Thomas Merton describes a life-changing mystical experience. Merton felt the unity of life in a transformative way as he walked the streets of Louisville, Kentucky. On a rare outing from the Trappist monastery at Gethsemani, Kentucky:

> at the corner of Fourth and Walnut, in the center of the shopping district, I was suddenly overwhelmed with the realization that I loved all those people, that they were mine and I was theirs, that we could not be alien to one another even though we were total strangers. It was like waking from a dream of separateness…The whole illusion of separate holy existence is a dream.[12]

Merton discovered that the sacred and secular were one in reality and that love connected him with all creation in all its amazing diversity. It is not accidental that in later life Merton championed human rights and opposed the military-industrial complex.

In this practice, we cultivate an experience of unity with all creation, including with those with whom we disagree politically. North African mystics say that the monk is "all eye". Moreover, the spiritual seeker is "all sense", intuiting the deeper unity beneath the many diversities of life.

This practice is an eyes-open form of mindfulness prayer. Begin your day with the following affirmations: "God, make me an

---

12   Thomas Merton, *Essential Writings* (Maryknoll, NY, 2000), 90.

instrument of your peace," "I see the unity of life," and "I see the world with the eyes of love."

Throughout the day, train your senses to experience your connection with everyone you meet. Look beneath the exterior differences to see the ultimate unity and connection. Notice the divinity within each person you meet. When you find yourself feeling alienated from someone, affirm "I see you with the eyes of love, we are one in the spirit." When you choose to challenge a political position of another person or call a congressional representative, experience your unity and make a commitment to experience your loving unity with them. Let love guide your words and actions.

5

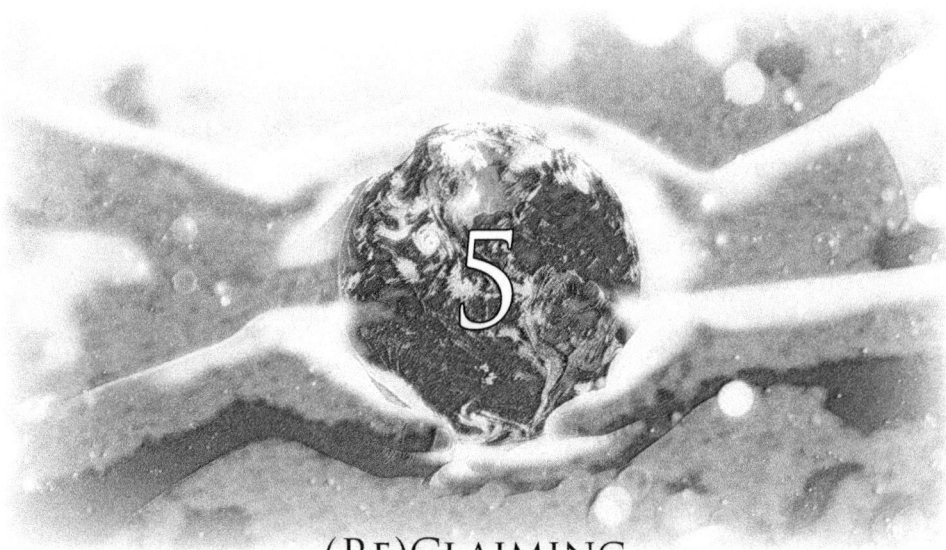

(Re)Claiming a Relationship with Jesus, the Healer, Mystic, and Prophet and The Spirit as Mystical Guide

Jesus came to Galilee proclaiming the good news of God and saying, "The time is fulfilled, and the kingdom of God has come near; repent, and believe in the good news."
(Mark 1:14-15)

And Jesus answered them, "Go and tell John what you have seen and heard: the blind receive their sight; the lame walk; those with a skin disease are cleansed; the deaf hear; the dead are raised; the poor have good news brought to them. And blessed is anyone who takes no offense at me."
(Luke 7:22-23)

Recently a friend of mine visited a United Church of Christ congregation for the first time. A recovering evangelical, now in the open and relational theology camp, she was pleased at the open-spirited theology and generous welcome. She planned to return in the future, but had one comment which I took to heart, "The denomination's name is United Church of Christ, but I didn't hear the name 'Jesus' or 'Christ' mentioned in the course of worship." My friend is spot on in her observation. Most progressive friends prefer to speak of "God" rather than "Jesus." Jesus has too much baggage and has been appropriated by those who see a datable conversion experience and a personal relationship with Jesus as the only path to salvation. Moreover, the Holy Spirit is seldom invoked in progressive congregations. My friend's comments raise the question: Are we missing something of importance in our reticence to invoke "Jesus" or the "Holy Spirit" in progressive Christianity in contrast to "evangelical" and "Pentecostal" Christians?

When progressives invoke the name of God, we are not excluding Jesus or the Holy Spirit. We tend to see God as the most global and inviting word in the context of a world in which religion, in particular doctrinal and authoritarian religion, is one of primary sources of violence and division. We also identify the constant invocation of Jesus and the Holy Spirit with more conservative and exclusivist forms of religion. As one of my friends complained, "When someone I know says, 'I've just accepted Jesus as my personal Savior," I become anxious. I anticipate that soon I will be hearing about the dangers of drag queens, homosexuality, Black Lives Matter, and socialism." Yet, loving Jesus and the awakening to the Holy Spirit need not be entryways to white Christian nationalism or unrestrained individualistic capitalism or the worship of Donald Trump as God's anointed emissary to lead the United States. Jesus should mean freedom, welcome, hospitality, and healing, and the Holy Spirit should mean unity amid diversity and openness to mystical experiences. We can be progressives who love Jesus, feel the movements of the spirit, raise our hands in worship and shout "Amen" as I do, and speak in tongues. Spiritual experiences don't come with a theological copyright! That copyright certainly doesn't belong to conservative or "evangelical" Christians, prosperity gospelers, or Trump Church!

We can reclaim Jesus and the Holy Spirit as central to our faith without embracing individualism, xenophobia, and conservatism. I believe that it is important for progressives to embrace the personal and mystical as well as universal aspects of God's nature and to join in a healthful fashion utter dependence on God, the power greater than ourselves in times of crisis, and our responsibility to be agents in bringing healing and justice to the planet. We can reclaim God in God's fullness as personal, relational, and transformational, both intimate and infinite.

What a Friend We Have in Jesus!

Too often progressive Christians, despite our proclamation of a historically involved God, are functional Deists, who affirm "if it's going to be, it's up to me." We don't want to "use" God for our own personal gain or to brow beat those with whom we disagree. Moreover, we don't want to be identified with Christians who constantly pray for supernatural intervention to solve their problems, cure illnesses, or win elections. For us, an uninvolved God is preferable to a micromanaging binary God just as an agnostic on the Supreme Court is likely a better choice than a fundamentalist or born again Christian in protecting the environment, democracy, and human rights.

Faith lives by what it affirms, not just what it denies. Progressive Christians need to formulate more inspirational alternative visions to the authoritarian micromanaging supernatural God. A truly Personal God more resembles a companion than a king, and mentor more than a dictator. From this perspective, God's love is responsive as well as creative, listening to and being shaped by us, adapting to our world, as well as being the source of healing possibilities. God may be, as Alfred North Whitehead says, "the fellow sufferer who understands." God may also be described as the joyful companion who celebrates and the intimate friend who inspires and challenges.

As a child growing up in an evangelical Baptist church, my faith was nurtured by hymns and carols. I am grateful for the evangelical hymns and traditional Christmas carols that are vital to my adult progressive faith. One of the old standbys of my childhood was "What a Friend We Have in Jesus." The words describe a God who is personal and not coercive, companionable without being supernatural, far from the authoritarian God of today's "evangelicals." Reflect on the words as an expression of relationship and acceptance, not doctrinal correctness and judgment. You might even listen to them on one of the music platforms.

> What a Friend we have in Jesus,
>   All our sins and griefs to bear!
> What a privilege to carry
>   Everything to God in prayer!
> O what peace we often forfeit,
>   O what needless pain we bear,
> All because we do not carry
>   Everything to God in prayer![13]

Christ is Alive! Jesus Lives On! Jesus is the friend of the soul, *anamcara,* as Celtic spiritual guides affirm. Christ hears our prayers and is touched by us! Christ is as near as our next breath! Not bound by space or time, but entangled in all things Jesus the Living One still shapes our lives. Awakening to the living Jesus changes our lives and opens us to new possibilities of relating to God and one another. Unlike the coercive and authoritarian Caesars of history, Jesus delights in our achievements and wants us to experience his energy, power, and creativity and share it with the world. The One who reveals God's vision in the flesh wants us to reveal that same vision in our bodies, minds, spirits, and relationships. Because Jesus is alive and has triumphed over the powers of death and destruction, we can expect great things from God and great things from one another. That is the Living Jesus' promise to us.

> *Very truly, I tell you, the one who believes in me will also do the works that I do and, in fact, will do greater works than these, because I am going to the Father. I will do whatever you ask in*

---

13 Joseph M. Scriven, 1855.

my name, so that the Father may be glorified in the Son. If in my name you ask me for anything, I will do it. (John 14:12-14)

In Christ, the Intimate and Infinite Face of God, Jesus calls us to walk with God in our daily lives and citizenship. Marching in the Light of God, we confront the dangers of our time with love and courage. Jesus the Christ is the heart beat of love, intimate and accepting. With a heart as wide as the universe, Jesus' love, like that of the Buddhist Bodhisattva, embraces all creation and will not cease in the quest for healing and wholeness until all creatures find salvation or wholeness.

Jesus as Mystical Companion

Marcus Borg describes Jesus as a "spirit person," one who experienced God as an intimate reality, and shared his mystical relationship with God with others. Relationship is at the heart of Jesus' mysticism. Jesus proclaimed, "I and the Father are one" and "the Father is in me, and I am in the Father" (John 10:30, 38). While we cannot fully describe Jesus' metaphysical unity with God, we can affirm that Jesus shared God's Spirit as his deepest reality. Jesus was a "thin place," transparent to Divinity. The Incarnation is the fullness of God in the life of Jesus, the revelation in his life of God's presence in all things. Fully Human, Jesus is the Glory of God, who enables us to realize our identity as God's "light of the world" (Matthew 5:14-16). The Incarnation is not a supernatural rescue operation, initiated by a distant God, but a naturalistic manifestation of the "God in whom we live and move and have our being" (Acts 17:28). Jesus is not "other" than us, but the revelation in flesh of what we are meant to be as God's beloved children.

The Incarnation of the Empathetic and Relational God, the Most Moved Mover, Jesus truly is one with us, feeling our joy and sorrow, beckoning us toward realizing who we can be as companions in God's Beloved Community. As the Christmas Carol, "Once in Royal David's City," proclaims:

For he is our childhood's pattern;
Day by day, like us He grew;
He was little, weak and helpless,
Tears and smiles like us He knew;
And He feeleth for our sadness,
And He shareth in our gladness.
And our eyes at last shall see Him,
Through His own redeeming love;
For that Child so dear and gentle
Is our Lord in heaven above,
And He leads His children on
To the place where He is gone.[14]

Open to God's moment by moment inspiration, which touches all creatures, and fully in synch with God's experience of the world, as we are in our most loving moments, we experience Jesus then and now is the revelation of the Energy of Love, mediating God's presence to all creation. We can look toward Jesus as our inspiration and call on Jesus to shape our lives and be our companion in the challenges we face. Aligned with Jesus, all moments can be "thin places," filled with divine grace, insight, and healing.

Jesus as Healing Presence

As a child, I learned the African American Spiritual, "There is a Balm in Gilead." Despite the brutality of slavery, African Americans trusted that God would have the final world. God's aim, in an oppressive society, is the healing of body, mind, and spirit, and also the body politic. Freedom and resilience for the long haul of justice seeking is God's goal for the oppressed and for those who seek social transformation, and God will provide a healing balm that transforms persons and communities.

There is a balm in a Gilead

---

14   Cecil Frances Alexander 1848

To heal the wounded soul.
There is a balm in Gilead
To heal the sin sick soul.[15]

The savior of the world is also the savior of our souls, not by rescuing us from the world, but through enabling us to discover the holiness of this world. God's eye is on the sparrow and I know God watches me. Jesus the healer experiences us intimately. God knows our joys and sorrows and works to bring healing to our lives and relationships. God's healing power is invitational and not coercive. God in Christ works through our bodies and minds, energizing a deeper naturalism, the Energy of Love. God's healing power works within our lives and not from a far-off heaven. The natural world is miraculous, and spiritual "thin places" reveal God's power in partnership with human openness to heal cells and souls. A personal God addresses each of us personally, and Jesus of Nazareth is the personal energy of God moving within each of our lives. Christ centers each of us personally and in that spiritual center energizes us and enables us to experience God's abundant life for us. Jesus is the healing presence in our personal lives and also the transforming presence of institutions and nations. The Prince of Peace challenges us to be peacemakers. The Galilean healer empowers us to create frameworks for healing and wholeness in our schools, congregations, communities, state and national governments, and the relationships of nations. Jesus the healer wants to prevent illness and encourage wellbeing and this requires life-supporting and justice-oriented institutions and governmental policies.

God in Christ has a personal relationship with each of us, even when we are not aware of it. This intimate presence invites us to call upon God as we would a parent or friend. "Our" parent or sibling knows us, loves us, and seeks our wholeness. We don't need supernatural intervention when we know that God is always with us. We don't need a datable Second Coming when we believe Jesus speaks to us every second. Nor do we need divine emissaries

15 19th century, author unknown

in the White House when we experience God inspiring all of us to do justice and love mercy and walk with humility. (Micah 6:8)

Jesus as Prophetic Challenge.

One of my favorite hymns from childhood and today is "Blessed Assurance." God's intimacy enables us to sing:

> Blessed assurance, Jesus is mine,
> O what a foretaste of glory divine…
> This is my story, this is my song,
>
> Praising my savior all the day long.[16]

A variation of this hymn asserts, "Blessed disturber, I am his." Jesus's first sermon, reflecting the wisdom of Isaiah, proclaimed:

> The Spirit of the Lord is upon me,
>   because he has anointed me
>   to bring good news to the poor.
> He has sent me to proclaim release to the captives
>   and recovery of sight to the blind,
>   to set free those who are oppressed,
>   to proclaim the year of the Lord's favor.
>   (Luke 4:18-19)

The hometown crowd is amazed and affirmative of Jesus' words until he proclaims God's blessing on everyone, including his nation's foes. The foe of every form of xenophobia, Jesus finds himself the object of the hatred of those who had just applauded his message. To xenophobes and homophobes, isolationists and nationalists, Jesus proclaims that God blesses every life, friend and foe, and every life can manifest God's blessing to the world (Luke 4:24-30).

---

16 Fanny Crosby, 1873

A child of the prophets, Jesus presented an alternative vision of reality, joining prayer and protest, contemplation and communal transformation. Jesus knew the meaning of oppression. He never lived a moment as a free person politically. His body was always at the disposal of the Roman oppressors, and the Romans, and their Jewish minions, forced Jesus to make the ultimate the sacrifice on Calvary. The Romans could control Jesus' body, but not his spirit. His spirit, joined with God's spirit, transcended and challenged every form of bondage and limitation. As the African American spiritual chants:

> I sing because I'm happy,
> I sing because I'm free,
> God's eye is on the sparrow,
> And I know God's watching me.[17]

Jesus joined prayer and prophetic ministry. Jesus' prophetic ministry was personal. The empathetic Jesus reflected the empathetic God. Jesus' intimacy mirrored God's intimacy. The word made flesh, Jesus felt pain and joy, betrayal and loyalty, anxiety and hope. Jesus was, and is, the asylum seeker, leaving home to escape death. Jesus was, and is, the innocent person unjustly punished. Jesus was, and is, the working poor, the trades person living month to month on a shrinking paycheck, and marginalized foreigner and the ostracized transgender youth. Jesus is on a journey with every "Jesús, María y José" traveling north from Central America. Jesus lived through every season of life and experienced every human emotion. Jesus is our "anamcara," the ultimate friend of the soul. We can come to Jesus in prayer, asking for guidance. We can reach out to Jesus in quest for a vision, asking "what would you do?" in response to injustice, racism, and climate denial. When we march prayerfully against injustice, we are marching in the light of God. Jesus marches against apartheid, homophobia, bombing in Gaza, and anti-Semitism in the United States. We can

---

17 Composer Charles Hutchison Gabriel and lyricist Silvila Durfy Martin, 1905

"take everything to God in prayer," knowing that Jesus searches us and knows us, and is our closest companion whether we are in the heights and depths and energizes us from the inside out and outside in to "let justice roll down like waters and righteousness like an ever-flowing stream" (Amos 5:24).

A Word About the Holy Spirit

The Holy Spirit is the unrestrained God. Within the Spirit, there are no boundaries. The Spirit is God's great "yes" to humankind in all its diversity. You can't exclude your neighbor and claim God's Spirit is with you. God's Spirit calls us to Pentecostal Transformation and Unity each moment, breaking down every barrier and tearing down every wall. The Holy Spirit doesn't provide explicit public policy initiatives related to immigration or reparation, but She tells us that whatever we do must aim at healing and reconciliation.

> *In the last days it will be, God declares,*
> *that I will pour out my Spirit upon all flesh,*
> *and your sons and your daughters shall prophesy,*
> *and your young men shall see visions,*
> *and your old men shall dream dreams.*
> *Even upon my slaves, both men and women,*
> *in those days I will pour out my Spirit,*
> *and they shall prophesy.* (Acts 2:17-18)

When we open to God's Spirit, expressed in Jesus' mission statement (Luke 4:18-19) and throughout this book, we know that there is a "sweet, sweet Spirit in this place," and this place is everywhere and welcoming to everyone. The Spirit speaks within us – and our churches – with "sighs too deep for words," calling us to hear Her voice in all things and help every creature find its voice as our companion in God's Beloved Community.

Nurturing a Robust and Activist Progressive Spirit

Jesus is as near as our next breath. Jesus is alive in our personal and political lives and challenges us to be companions in healing the world. In these exercises, we awaken to Christ as a companion and challenger. In claiming our relationship with Jesus, we are filled with Christ's Energy of Love, Creative Transformation, and Planetary Healing. In opening to God's Spirit, every breath entangles and joins us with all creation, and awakens us to our common identity as God's beloved children.

Kything, or Deep Empathy. At the heart of progressive spirituality is the affirmation that "there is no other." In the graceful interdependence of life, there are no strangers. Ubuntu, "I am because of you. We are because of one another." The Beloved Community of Jesus joins the energetic entanglement of all creation with the uniqueness of each creature. Accordingly, we can experience unity not only with "friends, foes, and strangers," but also our "good ancestors," the cloud of witnesses that surrounds us with love and that shaped and still shapes our lives. The "Great Ancestor" is Jesus the Christ whose Spirit enlivens us with every breath. The Incarnate Risen Jesus is alive today in our hearts and the world, softly and tenderly and sometimes boldly and energetically calling us to be his companions in saving the world.

One way to encounter the living Jesus is through visualizing Jesus as your constant companion through a process called "kything." Grounded in a Scottish word coined by Madeleine L'Engle, kything is "a spiritual act of conscious presence" with another across time and space.[18] As I noted earlier, the graceful interdependence of life joins every creature. Non- local in nature and joining us despite physical distance, kything is "spirit-to-spirit" presence.[19] In kything, we experience our empathetic communication with all creation as it is focused on a particular relation-

---

18 Louis Savary and Patrician Berne, *Kything: The Art of Spiritual Presence* (Mahwah, NJ: Paulist Press, 1988), 7.

19 Ibid., 17.

ship. This form of empathetic understanding, or spiritual unity, involves a flexible three-step process: 1) centering through breath or focus, 2) focusing imaginatively or empathetically on another, perhaps through visualization of the one whom you wish to contact, and 3) establishing a spiritual connection or union through awareness of companionship across space and time. When I kythe, a practice similar to intercessory prayer, I visualize the other beside me, spiritually joined, and sharing love with one another. We are one in the Spirit and at a deep unconscious level, we are connected even beyond the grave.

While you may focus on any person in your life, living or among the ancestors, I invite you to "kythe" with Jesus. Visualize Jesus beside you, in conversation, sharing a task, or walking, similar to the Emmaus Road experience. I regularly take Jesus on my morning walk. I visualize him walking beside me, fully present, and sharing wisdom. Sometimes I put my arm around my "imaginary friend," only to discover the energy and wisdom of his presence flowing into and through my mind, body, and spirit.

Singing with Jesus. Augustine of Hippo, the North African theologian and mystic, is reputed to have said that "singing is praying twice." Indeed, singing is a whole person activity that joins body, mind, spirit, and relationships. Growing up I was taught to sing the hymn "Living for Jesus" as a prayer. It still inspires me.

> Living for Jesus a life that is true,
> striving to please him in all that I do,
> yielding allegiance, glad-hearted and free,
> this is the pathway of blessing for me.
> O Jesus, Lord and Savior, I give myself to thee,
> for thou, in thy redemption, didst give thyself for me;
> I own no other master, my heart shall be thy throne,
> my life I give, henceforth to live,
> O Christ, for thee alone.[20]

---

20   Thomas Chisholm and Carl Harold Lowden, "Living for Jesus," 1917

In the dynamic call and response of life, Jesus sacrifices for me, embraces me, invites me to live for him, and follow his path of love. Truly Jesus loves me, and in return I love him by loving the world for which he sacrificed. We don't need to worry about the many doctrines of atonement, nor do we need to affirm that Jesus died in our place to enable us to escape a vindictive god's wrath. Rather, Jesus' sacrificial love for creation inspires me to live a life of empathy, sacrifice, and love.

In this spiritual practice, I invite you to live with four hymns that invite us to walk in the way of Jesus with Jesus as our Friend and Companion. Over a period of three days, take time throughout the day to read the words and then listen contemplatively to each hymn (there are many versions of each on music platforms), letting the interplay of words and music speak to your spirit. On the fourth day, we invoke God's restless, iconoclastic, and healing Spirit. You may choose to sing them throughout the day. Since the first three are "walking hymns" focusing on God as a companion, guide, and protector, you might choose to take a walk, contemplating what it would be like to have Jesus walk with you. If walking presents a challenge, visualize Jesus by your side throughout the day. Prayerfully ask, in the style of *lectio divina*, "What is the meaning of this hymn in my life? What is God saying to me in these hymns? If I let these hymns guide me, how would my personal, relational, and political life be transformed?"

Day One: "I Want Jesus to Walk with Me." Contemplate these words as they relate to your life and your desire to have Jesus as your companion on the walk of life:

> I want Jesus to walk with me.
> I want Jesus to walk with me;
> all along my pilgrim journey,
> Lord, I want Jesus to walk with me.
> In my trials, Lord, walk with me.
> In my trials, Lord, walk with me;
> when my heart is almost breaking,

Lord, I want Jesus to walk with me.
When I'm in trouble, Lord, walk with me.
When I'm in trouble, Lord, walk with me;
when my head is bowed in sorrow,
Lord, I want Jesus to walk with me.[21]

Imagine asking Jesus to be your companion and then experiencing joining you as you walk through life. Where is Jesus walking with you now? Where do you need to wake up to Jesus' companionship on your life's journey?

Day Two: "O Master (or Jesus), Let Me Walk with Thee." Whereas the first hymn invoked Jesus' companionship, this hymn asks for Jesus to invite me to walk with him, or for me to endeavor to be Jesus' companion. I want to walk with Jesus concretely in my life. Contemplate these words as they relate to your life and your desire to join Jesus in your quest to be a contemplative activist. Ponder Abraham Heschel's comment after marching for justice with Martin Luther King, "I felt like my legs were praying." If you are physically able, take a walk as you listen to or meditate on the meaning of this hymn. If physical movement is challenging to you, you can visualize yourself walking through your daily tasks with Jesus as your companion. In so doing, you seek to mediate God's presence to those around you.

O Master, let me walk with Thee,
In lowly paths of service free;
Tell me Thy secret; help me bear
The strain of toil, the fret of care.
Help me the slow of heart to move
By some clear, winning word of love;
Teach me the wayward feet to stay,
And guide them in the homeward way.
Teach me Thy patience; still with Thee
In closer, dearer, company,

---

21   African American Spiritual (public domain), Adapted by William Farley
     Smith

In work that keeps faith sweet and strong,
In trust that triumphs over wrong.
In hope that sends a shining ray
Far down the future's broad'ning way,
In peace that only Thou canst give,
With Thee, O Master, let me live.[22]

Throughout the day, you might choose to visualize Jesus as your companion, gently guiding you on paths of righteousness. With Jesus beside you, you are never alone nor can you be defeated by life's temptations or the forces of evil.

Day Three – "We are Marching in the Light of God." Listen to this song of freedom as you repeat it over and over again. You may choose to march and sing as you contemplate. You may also choose to add words: "we are living in the light of God…we are loving in the light of God…we are dancing in the light of God… we are praying in the light of God…we are healing in the light of God…we protest in the light of God." March forward with Jesus, letting your legs pray as you move along.

Day Four – "Spirit of Gentleness." God's Spirit comforts, challenges, and transforms. God's Spirit is the inner witness that connects us with the external world, creatively entangling us with the fate of our fellow humans and the fate of the earth. The Gentle Spirit is the Prophetic Spirit, seeking liberty and justice for all, and affirming the image of God in everyone personally and politically. Let the Spirit of the Living God, fall afresh on us, as we live with Jim Manley's hymn:

Spirit, Spirit of gentleness,
blow through the wilderness calling and free,
Spirit, Spirit of restlessness,
stir me from placidness,
wind, wind on the sea.

---

22 Washington Gladden, "O Master, Let Me Walk with Thee." (public domain)

You moved on the waters,
you called to the deep,
then you coaxed up the mountains
from the valleys of sleep;
and over the eons you called to each thing:
"Awake from your slumbers
and rise on your wings."
You swept through the desert,
you stung with the sand,
and you goaded your people with a law and a land;
and when they were blinded
with idols and lies,
then you spoke through your prophets
to open their eyes.
You sang in a stable,
you cried from a hill,
then you whispered in silence
when the whole world was still;
and down in the city
you called once again,
when you blew through your people
on the rush of the wind.
You call from tomorrow,
you break ancient schemes.
From the bondage of sorrow
all the captives dream dreams;
our women see visions,
our men clear their eyes.
With bold new decisions
your people arise.[23]

Filled with the Spirit, and walking with Jesus as our Companion, "how can we keep from singing?"

---

23   Jim Manley, "Spirit of Gentleness."

6

BECOMING MYSTICS IN ACTION

God is our refuge and strength,
a very present help in trouble.
Therefore we will not fear, though the earth should change,
though the mountains shake in the heart of the sea,
though its waters roar and foam,
though the mountains tremble with its tumult.

There is a river whose streams make glad the city of God,
the holy habitation of the Most High.
God is in the midst of the city; it shall not be moved;
God will help it when the morning dawns.
The nations are in an uproar; the kingdoms totter;
he utters his voice; the earth melts.
The LORD of hosts is with us;
the God of Jacob is our refuge.

Come, behold the works of the LORD;
see what desolations he has brought on the earth.
He makes wars cease to the end of the earth;
he breaks the bow and shatters the spear;
he burns the shields with fire.
"Be still, and know that I am God!

I am exalted among the nations;
I am exalted in the earth."
The LORD of hosts is with us;
the God of Jacob is our refuge (Psalm 46)

The Christian of the future will be a mystic, or [they]
shall not exist atall. (Karl Rahner)

The world we live in these days mirrors the challenges de-scribed in Psalm 46. The body politic trembles. Domestic terrorists storm the Capitol, hellbent on undermining the peaceful transition of presidential power for which the United States has boasted since Washington left office in 1797. The rule of law is flouted by "law and order" citizens. Lies are taken for truth, and conservative Christians willingly embrace conspiracy theories and worship a prevaricating, dishonest, and morally bankrupt politician as if he is the Second Coming of Jesus. The non-human world mirrors the chaos and aimlessness of humanity. Forest fires and hurricanes demonstrate the impact of climate change. Icebergs melt and collapse, and the sea rises. Islands in the Indian Ocean and Pacific are on the verge of being overwhelmed by rising waters. Millions of persons are climate refugees and we can only anticipate millions more, dwarfing the current immigration on the USA border. We are in a time of upheaval and fear the survival not only of democracy but of the planet as climate deniers, whose mantra is "drill, drill, drill," seek to lead the USA.

The threat of national collapse was real then and is real now. Yet, without denying the threat, the Psalmist sees themself as the still center of the cyclone. The Psalmist's calm amid the storm is reminiscent of the tale of the night of falling stars. Observing a meteor shower, the citizens of the village panic. They run to and fro, shouting "the sky is falling, the sky is falling." Worn out from their sprinting, they pause at the home of the wise ones of the village. When the wise ones come outside, the crowd shares their fears of destruction. The wise ones reply, "Yes, the stars are falling. But, look at the stars that remain in place."

The source of calm is trust in the deeper and wider realities of life. Yes, we are in upheaval. The future of democracy is in doubt and many of our Christian kin are at the heart of the problem. But God is faithful. "God is in the midst of the city; it shall not be moved; God will help it when the morning dawns. The Lord of hosts is with us. The God of Jacob is our refuge." We find peace when we realize, with the African American spiritual,

> We've come this far by faith,
> Leaning on the Lord.
> Trusting in his holy word.
> He's never failed us yet.
> Oh, oh- oh- can't turn around,
> We've come this far by faith.[24]

In the stillness of contemplative prayer, the Psalmist experiences peace in the storm. "Be still and know that I am God." In quiet, the Psalmist hears the deep assurance of God, who will outlast every foe and heal every rift. God is God and we aren't, and that is a source of comfort and confidence. God will have the final word and that is peace and healing.

Progressive Christianity as a Laboratory for Holistic and Affirmative Mysticism

The interplay of theology, spirituality, and social action is at the heart of a progressive Christian revival. Our future as a movement for wholeness and unity depends on dynamic contemplative activism emerging from our congregations and influencing public policy and the tone of civil discourse. It has been said that faith is caught not taught. Grace abounds and God addresses us every millisecond, seeking our wholeness and salvation. Persons in our lives show us what it means to be a follower of Jesus. Or, we

---

24   "We've Come This Far by Faith," Albert A. Goodson (1956).

are simply born as Christians, finding meaning in a relationship
with Jesus in our mother's, father's, grandparents', and significant
others' arms. Life is a call and response, and like Samuel, Isaiah,
Mary of Nazareth, Mary of Magdala, and the apostle Paul, we
hear God's call, sometimes dramatically and other times subtly in
everyday events, and respond with a clear or implicit "yes." There
are moments for every person and nation in which God calls and
we respond, and on that response the future depends.

It is also true that faith is taught as well as caught. We need
to grow in wisdom and stature as children and as adults. We need
to experience the faith that is appropriate to our age, maturity,
responsibilities, and season of life. The growth of faith comes
through prayer and study, and, as our Jewish kin remind us, study
is a form of prayer. God constantly lures us to wider and deeper
faith, to a faith that is wise, experiential, and responsible to the
world. In a previous chapter, I asserted the importance of the interplay of theological reflection and spiritual practice in a healthy
and socially transformative faith. Our images of God incline us
toward social and political agency or passivity, democracy or authoritarianism, and hospitality or exclusion. Progressive churches
must emphasize the importance of world-affirming and socially
responsible theological education. Every congregation should be a
seminary and retreat house in miniature, where the stories of God
are shared, and we learn to say "yes" to certain theological and
ethical viewpoints and, accordingly, say "no" to others.

The church should also be a laboratory for world-affirming,
socially responsible, and whole person spirituality. While I am
grateful for the rise of centers for Christian spirituality such as
Richard Rohr's Center for Contemplation and Action and Washington DC's Shalem Institute for Spiritual Formation, where persons can learn the arts of prayer and meditation, congregations are
also challenged to join spirituality and social concern as essential
to their mission. We cannot leave spirituality or theology to others; we must practice holistic theology and spirituality in our congregations as essential to world-affirming faith.

The great religious traditions of the world had their origins and still find their wellsprings in mystical experiences. Indeed, if God is present in every encounter and every moment of life, then we are all mystics in the making. We are all touched by God. We all hear, deep down, the still, small voice of God, and we can pause and know that God is present in our lives and the world, coming to us with comfort, possibility, insight, and challenge. We are no different, except historically and contextually, from the great heroes of scripture and each one of us at childbirth bears, as Pelagius says, the face of God. We can be the Isaiahs, Amoses, Marys, Pauls, of our time. We can embody the spirit of Francis and Clare of Assisi, Julian of Norwich, Hildegard of Bingen, George Fox, Albert Schweitzer, Mother (Saint) Teresa, and Howard Thurman, and other great mystics of our faith and the world's religions in our own unique way for just a time as this.

While it is not my intent to provide a smorgasbord of spiritual practices in this text, my challenge is for each congregation or community of congregations to join theology, spirituality, and prophetic faith to transform and save the world in partnership with God. Although I will provide resources at the end of this chapter, it is important for me simply to present an image of holistic and vital spirituality for congregational life and social and political responsibility. The spirituality we need must be holistic and affirmative, to use the language of Quaker mystic-activist Rufus Jones. It must be a spirituality of involvement, not escape. Embodiment, not body denial. Community, not individualism. Global responsibility, not retreat from the world. It must be a spirituality that teaches us to pray and protest, contemplate and challenge, meditate and motivate, and understand and unite.

Jesus' disciples once asked, "Lord, teach us to pray." In response, Jesus taught them the Lord's prayer, inviting them to pray "your kingdom [kindom] come," (Luke 11:2) words elaborated in Matthew's version, "your kingdom [kindom] come on earth as it is in heaven" (Matthew 6:9-13) and remember that God is "our" Father/Parent, the parent of us all. We pray for God's realm

to be mirrored in our earthly lives and that means that we seek
to become persons of spirit whose prayers eventuate in protest,
picketing, and political responsibility as well as personal acts of
kindness. Spirituality drives us from solitude to society just as Jesus, following his retreat desert, returned to his community with
these words of vocation and challenge that should be central to
progressive Christianity, bearing repetition and contemplation:

> *The Spirit of the Lord is upon me,*
>   *because he has anointed me*
> *to bring good news to the poor.*
> *He has sent me to proclaim release to the captives*
>   *and recovery of sight to the blind,*
>   *to set free those who are oppressed,*
> *to proclaim the year of the Lord's favor.* (Luke 4:18-19)

Our spiritual lives invite us to holistic living, joining mind,
body, spirit, and hands and heart, to promote our own and others'
wellbeing. Our spiritual lives deepen our sense of peace, reduce
the stresses of our busy and socially responsible lives, and give us
patience and energy for the long road to national and planetary
healing. Our spiritual lives invite us to widen our imagination,
vision, and empathy. We discover that there is no "other" foreign
to ourselves. We are one in the spirit, even with those whom we
oppose. There is something divine in everyone, even those whom
we must challenge. We encounter Christ everywhere and in everyone and our spiritual pilgrimage involves seeing Christ, being
Christ, and bringing forth Christ in us and every situation. Our
faith is completed by vision and action, by prayer and service,
and contemplation and challenge. Moses heard God's voice in a
burning bush and became a national liberator. Isaiah encountered
God in the Temple and discovered his vocation as a prophet to
the nations. Mary of Nazareth encountered an angel, welcomed
an amazing birth, and preached about an upside-down economic
system in which the poor are uplifted and the wealthy let go of
power and property. We can see Christ and be Christ, claiming

our vocation as the hands and feet of our savior and liberator, who do greater things in our time to heal broken persons and broken systems not for our own self-aggrandizement or power but out of sacrificial and relational alignment with God's vision. Contemplation leads to action which unites, heals, and transforms. Action that does something beautiful for God by bringing beauty to the lives of others.

> *Then the king will say to those at his right hand, "Come, you who are blessed by my Father, inherit the kingdom prepared for you from the foundation of the world, for I was hungry and you gave me food, I was thirsty and you gave me something to drink, I was a stranger and you welcomed me, I was naked and you gave me clothing, I was sick and you took care of me, I was in prison and you visited me." Then the righteous will answer him, "Lord, when was it that we saw you hungry and gave you food or thirsty and gave you something to drink? And when was it that we saw you a stranger and welcomed you or naked and gave you clothing? And when was it that we saw you sick or in prison and visited you?" And the king will answer them, "Truly I tell you, just as you did it to one of the least of these brothers and sisters of mine, you did it to me."* (Matthew 25:34-40)

Nurturing a Robust and Activist Progressive Spirit

Theology, spirituality, and social transformation emerge in dynamic process of creative transformation, integrating a dynamic divine call and an equally dynamic human response that deepens our faith and widens our compassion for the long haul. We come to resemble in our own empathy God's empathy toward all creation. We also come to embody God's prophetic vision in seeking to bring heaven to earth and Shalom to everyday life. A.J. Muste once said "There is no way to peace; peace is the way." The same applies to spirituality. While our spiritual lives join grace and effort, call and response, we become spiritual persons by practicing spirituality in every situation, whether in solitude or community. Accordingly, there are many spiritual practices, suited to every season and situation of life. In this section, I will share a few of the many spiritual practices that many progressive Christians have found helpful that quest for holistic, socially responsible faith, and in the spiritual journeys of friends and companions.

The Breath of Life. Breath is central in experiencing wholeness, calm, and community. Breath calms, energizes, connects, and gives us resilience for the long haul of justice-seeking and planet-protecting. Noted earlier, pastor-activist Allan Armstrong Hunter taught a breath prayer, in which we breathed deeply God's Spirit and then sent it peacefully out in the world. Filled with the Spirit, we shared God's Spirit with others. In this exercise, begin by reading Hunter's poem to accompany this meditation as you breathe slowly and evenly:

> I breathe your blue sky deeply in
> To blow it gladly back again.
> I breathe your shining beauty in
> To call forth the buried talent in me.
> I breathe your healing energy in
> To vibrate through each body cell.
> We breathe your reconciling spirit in
> To bring peace in us, and in the world.
> We breathe your resurrection power in
> To make our relationships new and glad.
> We breathe your strength and warmth and humor in
> To share joyously with all we meet.

As you breathe deeply, feel your connection with all things, recognizing that deep down, despite our current binary political and cultural divide, there is no other. Breathe out a sense of peace and connection to all you meet. Take a few minutes each day for this breath prayer. Return to the breath prayer if you feel alienated or anxious. Let it fill you with calm and peace to respond to the injustice and alienation of our world.

Listen to Your Children Praying. Christian singer-song writer Ken Medema sings "Lord, listen to your children praying," and then asks that God fill our congregations with God's Spirit to fill us with "power, love, and grace." When we pray, the walls of separation and injustice come tumbling down. In this spiritual practice, listen to a version of Ken Medema's song. Then ponder the brokenness of the world. Perhaps, you might choose to see images of children in your neighborhood, in far off cities and rural areas, in wealth and poverty, playing joyfully in gyms, back yards, and fields, and also fleeing violence. Perhaps, you might look at images of immigrant and refugee children as well as children in Gaza, Ukraine, Sudan, Palestine, Israel, and other war-torn lands. Pray for these children and then vow to be an answer to your prayers by doing acts of justice and healing personally, through your congregation, and through speaking to your political representatives.

Circles of Light. In a variation on the breath prayer, breathe deeply God's light. Let it fill your cells and souls, bringing healing, energy, and enlightenment. As you breathe out, let your breath expand in circles beginning with yourself and radiating to your closest companions, congregation, community, state, nation, planet, and, as Buzz Lightyear from "Toy Story" proclaims, "to infinity and beyond." Feel the light healing your spirit and contributing to the healing of each of these circles. Give thanks for the opportunity to be God's companion in healing the earth.

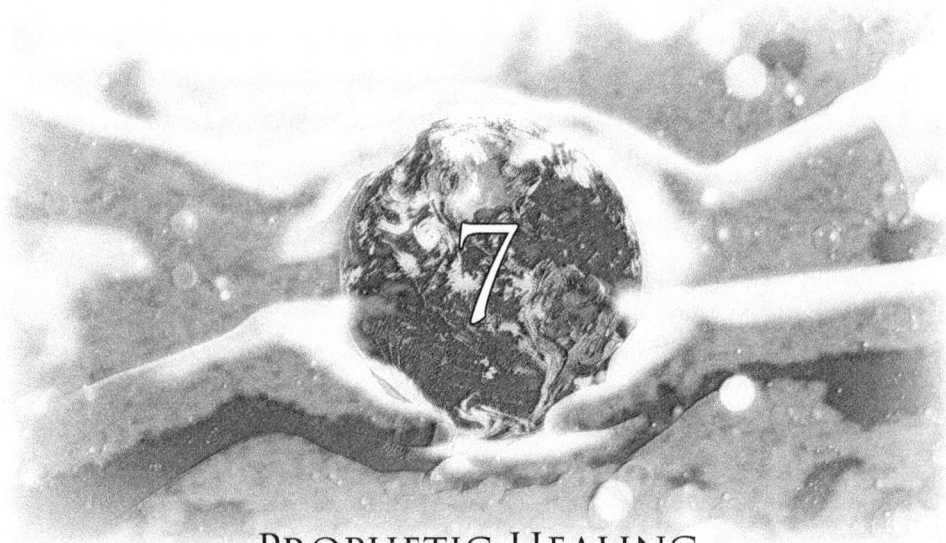

PROPHETIC HEALING

The wilderness and the dry land shall be glad;
the desert shall rejoice and blossom;
like the crocus it shall blossom abundantly
and rejoice with joy and shouting.
The glory of Lebanon shall be given to it,
the majesty of Carmel and Sharon.
They shall see the glory of the LORD,
the majesty of our God. (Isaiah 35:1-2)

In the ancient world, spirituality, politics, and healing were interdependent. Moses' mystical experience endowed him with spiritual power and a political vision aimed at healing an oppressed people. Isaiah encounters God in the Jerusalem Temple, and out of his mystical experience of God's majesty receives the calling to be a prophet of a new era of justice and peace. Although our savior and healer Jesus lived under the oppressive rule of Rome, his unity with God gave him the power to heal bodies, minds, spirits, and relationships. While not a political document in the narrow sense of the word, the Sermon on the Mount (Matthew, chapters 5-7) challenges Christians who claim to follow Jesus to pattern their civic leadership and political involvement according to God's realm "on earth as it is in heaven," focusing on a politics of inclusion, reconciliation, affirmation, servanthood, and reverence for life. Although the early Christian community lacked political power and was often the victim of persecution, the body of Christ sought to promote equality among all its members, ensure economic well being for everyone in the community, encourage sacrificial living, shared resources, and the realization of each member's gifts as well as generosity to strangers. Within the Christian community, diversity came to be seen as a gift, religious boundaries were overcome, and foreigners were treated as God's beloved children, created in God's image and redeemed by Jesus' love.

When we enter the realm of politics, followers of Jesus are challenged to be both prophetic witnesses and healers, following Jesus' initial sermon and mission statement, the mantra for the integration of spirituality and social transformation for Progressive Christianity cited throughout this text. (Luke 4:18-19) We may choose to protest, resist, and practice civil disobedience, but always with the aim at healing persons and institutions, at recovering the soul of the nation and bringing good news to oppressed and oppressor alike.

Jesus' mission statement from Luke's Gospel is a text to live by every day and so central to the progressive Christian vision that it bears daily repetition as we seek to be God's companions in creating a just, beautiful, hospitable, healthy, and inclusive body politic where the poor receive good news, captives are set free, the blind experience healing, the oppressed find justice, and God's realm of wholeness becomes an everyday reality.

Noted earlier in this text. Jesus' initial audience may have noticed that Jesus omitted the word "vengeance," invoked by the prophet Isaiah. Jesus' words were applauded by his townsfolk until he asserted that God's grace was universal, coming to all people and not just his religious and ethnic kin. Angered by Jesus' open source and universal vision of God's love and empowerment, the crowd sought to kill him. (Luke 4:24-30) In Jesus' realm, there are no outsiders, no "vermin" who "poison our blood." Outsiders and sinners – those who are outside our community, persons considered unclean or different than ourselves – are to be welcomed as kin and God's beloved children. Even agents of the Empire were embraced by Jesus' love. Healing and transformation are offered to everyone from the MAGA insurrectionist to the asylum seeker they fear.

The Prophetic Spirit

While opposing any form of theocracy, dominion theology, or Apostolic Reformation in which "traditional" Christian legalism becomes the basis for law, progressive Christianity is prophetic by nature. Progressive Christians are the children of the Social Gospel movement, which sought to embody the values of Jesus in economics and at the workplace. Many things that we take for granted today were at the heart of the Social Gospel vision: forty-hour work week, holidays and days off, safe working conditions, decent salaries, and workers' rights. Roosevelt's New Deal reflected the impact of religious and secular groups who believed that government had a positive role in promoting personal and national wellbeing. It was the job of government to feed the hungry, care for the earth, and ensure equal access to the American dream. Indeed, the Biblical and Progressive spirit sees government as a vehicle of healing, justice, and inclusion, and not merely an evil to restrain vice. The prophets yearned for a big enough government to address injustice and promote social well being, and so do we!

Today's progressive Christians embrace the social vision of Jesus and Jewish prophetic tradition. At the heart of the prophetic vision is the interplay of empathy and possibility. Abraham Joshua Heschel identifies the *divine pathos* as the central insight of the prophets, in which God "does not reveal himself in absolute abstractness, but in personal and intimate relationship to the world. He does not simply command and expect obedience; [God] is also moved and affected by what happens in the world and reacts accordingly. Events and human actions arouse in [God] joy or

sorrow, pleasure or wrath."[25]   What happens in the world matters to God. God is the Ultimate Empath, feeling the currents of
our personal, national, and planetary history as if it is God's own
experience. God feels the pain of economic injustice, racism and
inequality, poverty and violence, and environmental destruction.
God's eye is on the sparrow and God is watching you and me.
God feels the terror of a family fleeing Central America with hope
a better life in the United States. God feels the misplaced fear of
white Christian nationalists and Trump supporters, manipulated
by politicians, who describe asylum seekers as thugs, rapists, and
drug dealers. God experiences the celebration of parents whose
child is the first member of the family to attend college and the
elation of the LGBTQ+ families when marriage equality was legal-
ized and when gay and lesbian couples are able to adopt children.
The growing disparity between the rich and poor matters to God,
and the hopelessness and substance use addiction in urban areas
and Appalachia breaks God's heart. As Heschel claims, "the rabbis
were not guilty of exaggeration in asserting, 'Whoever destroys a
single soul should be considered the same as one who destroyed
a whole world. And whoever saves one single soul should be considered the same as one who has saved a whole world.'"[26]   While
maintaining the humility that comes with recognizing their common fallible humanity, the prophets see the world from the point
of view of God. They also feel the divine empathy, God's pain at
illness, injustice, and violence, much of which is the result of personal and institutional decision-making. Just as God constantly
influences our lives, whatever we do also affects God's experience.
"Pathos means: God is never neutral, never beyond good and evil.
He is always partial to justice."[27]   God has a preferential option
for the poor and honors those who see God's presence in the least
of these. We need, the prophets believed, a politics of the micro
and macro: a care for interpersonal relations and reverence for our

25   Abraham Joshua Heschel, *The Prophets* (Peabody, MA: Hendrickson,
     1962), volume 2, 3-4. (author's paraphrase)
26   Ibid., volume 1, 14.
27   Ibidl, vol. 2, 11.

neighbors and strangers and the national and planetary establishment of frameworks for justice and social welfare.

God seeks justice and so should we. Individualism, isolation, and unrestrained capitalism go against God's vision for humankind. Climate denial by Christians, mesmerized by false science and manipulative politicians, defies God's aspiration for the realization of the Peaceable Realm.

God is the ultimate source of novelty, adventure, imagination, and the restless quest for Beloved Community. God is the ultimate challenger to the status quo. The source of the moral and spiritual arcs of history, God inspires the quest for justice and healing. We cannot be content with injustice, must join in God's quest to repair the world. Popularized by Robert F. Kennedy, George Bernard Shaw describes the divine restlessness at injustice: "There are those that look at things the way they are, and ask why? I dream of things that never were, and ask why not?"

Theologian and First Testament scholar Walter Brueggemann asserts that prophetic ministry involves "direct, confrontational encounter with established power," whether religious, economic, or political.[28] Words matter, and prophets are wordsmiths, whose prophetic speech enables us to envision alternative worlds and open to both the hope and threat of imaginative futures. The prophetic critique of the present order of things emerges from their experience of divine pain and possibility. Inspired by God's vision of a Peaceable Realm, "the task of prophetic ministry [whether in Israel, Great Britain, Canada, or the United States] is to nurture, nourish, and evoke a consciousness and perception alternative to the consciousness and perception of the dominant culture around us."[29] The prophet proclaims a spiritual alternative to the "religion of static triumphalism and the politics of oppression and exploitation."[30] Jesus told his followers that they could do "greater things," and our congregations as communities of faithful persons

28 Walter Brueggemann, *The Prophetic Imagination* (Minneapolis: Fortress Press, 2001), ix.

29 Ibid., 3.

30 Ibid., 5.

can do greater things than we can imagine to heal the earth and promote just laws and economics. In the quest for God's realm of Shalom, the prophets tell us to expect great things from God and great things from ourselves in transforming our nation and the world.

Prophetic ministry goes hand in hand with spiritual growth and commitment to the way of Jesus. A personal relationship with Jesus binds us to the world God loves. Loving Jesus inspires incarnational living in the midst of life's challenges not escapism or world denial. Loving Jesus awakens us to his all-encompassing love and inspires us to abandon individualism, self-interest, and nationalism, for world loyalty, even as we secure the rights and liberty of every individual. God loves the world and calls us to do likewise by loving God's children in all their diversity, embracing as well as challenging those who perpetuate in justice, and expanding our care to include the non-human world.

As prophetic progressives we are to be active in the world without being caught up in the power plays and invective epidemic in politics, even among progressives. We are to be embedded in the world, feeling pain and seeking justice; but not conformed to the world's individualistic and consumerist values. In the world, all persons are kin. Yet, we are not to be caught up in the "worldly" temptations to incivility, binary thinking, injustice, consumerism, racism, and isolationism. We can love God and the world and be God's companions in healing the world God loves one act at a time and in our challenging of corporate and institutional injustice wherever we find it. Ironically, heavenly minded conservative Christians have carved out political policies and support candidates whose primary concern is this-worldly power, unrestrained capitalism, and control of immigrant, LGBTQ+, women's, and persons of color's bodies. Domination and coercive power are not the way of Christians who love the world God created and loves. We must love the world and humankind, work for life-affirming public policy, place world loyalty on par with national patriotism, and also cultivate non-attachment to particular programs and political groups even as we promote them.

Prophetic Healing

Revolutions often fail because they succumb to us-them, win-lose, good-evil ideologies that resemble the ideologies of the authoritarian and unjust regimes they seek to replace. Binary, power-oriented, political and theological approaches tend to demonize our opponents verbally and, then, often politically and judicially. Tragically, revolutions are often as bloodthirsty as the regimes they replace, for example, in Russia, China, North Korea, and Venezuela. In contrast, prophetic spirituality presents a conciliatory alternative to institutional injustice. Despite the need, at times, for intense and confrontive rhetoric, prophetic spirituality also presents an alternative path to securing justice.

The prophets have harsh words against predatory lenders, landowners, and unrestrained capitalism. Today, the prophets would be spearheading some form of safety net capitalism or common good economics. Yet, the prophetic protest is guided by an affirmative spirituality that seeks to embrace everyone. The prophet Amos proclaims: "let justice roll down like water and righteousness like an ever-flowing stream." (Amos 5:24) The prophet Micah counsels,

> He has told you, O mortal, what is good,
>   and what does the LORD require of you
> but to do justice and to love kindness
> and to walk humbly with your God? (Micah 6:8)

A profound critic of economic injustice and institutional idolatry, the prophet Isaiah dreams of a peaceable realm that heals the enmity in nature and human life and embraces the wellbeing of the whole earth and its diverse nations and peoples as well as our nation.

The wolf shall live with the lamb;
the leopard shall lie down with the kid;
the calf and the lion will feed together,
and a little child shall lead them.
The cow and the bear shall graze;
their young shall lie down together;
and the lion shall eat straw like the ox.
The nursing child shall play over the hole of the asp,
and the weaned child shall put its hand on the adder's den.
They will not hurt or destroy
on all my holy mountain,
for the earth will be full of the knowledge of the LORD
as the waters cover the sea. (Isaiah 11:6-9)

Is it possible to "do justice and to love kindness and to walk humbly with our God" in the scrum of protest and politics? No modern theologian has expressed the vision of prophetic healing better than African American mystic, theologian, and pastor Howard Thurman. Thurman will be our guide in a spiritually inspired process of prophetic healing. The grandson of slaves, Thurman grew up in the Jim Crow South, where the African Americans were subject to the institutional brutality of racism. Yet, Thurman found spiritual transcendence in mystical experiences. He did not forsake the quest for justice. In fact, Thurman's *Jesus and the Disinherited* may have been the first text in African American liberation theology. Martin Luther King carried Thurman's book in his satchel as a spiritual guide in his quest for the Beloved Community through non-violent resistance and civil disobedience. Thurman's vision was inspired by the power of love, not the love of power; the quest for healing the nation, not vanquishing the opponent.

As our guide to prophetic healing, Thurman joined mysticism and social action. A student of Quaker mystic Rufus Jones, Thurman taught an "affirmative mysticism" that soared to the heavens and then returned to the earth, to bring heavenly values to earthly communities. Thurman saw mystical experience as both heavenly minded and earthly good. According to Thurman, "mysticism is defined as the response of the individual to a personal encounter with God within his own soul. This is my working definition. Such a response is total, affecting the inner quality of life and its outward expression."[31] Contemplation inspires social transformation. Having experienced God as the source of creation in its wondrous multiplicity, the mystic desires that all people experience this same sense of wholeness, according to their unique personalities, cultures, and life-experiences. Thurman believes that when mystics observe conditions that threaten persons' encounters with God, they feel compelled to confront them. The mystic knows that injustice, racism, and institutional violence stifles the imagination, dampens dreams, traumatizes spirits, and forces people to focus on mere survival rather than spiritual fulfillment. "Social action, therefore, is an expression of resistance against whatever tends to, or separates one, from the experience of God, who is the ground of his being."[32] A spiritually oriented congregation creates a communion of contemplative activists, who join together to challenge injustice wherever it is found, even within their own congregations and denominations.

Spiritual and political commitments complement and complete each other, personally and congregationally. "For the mystic [and the mystical community], social action is sacramental, because it is not an end in itself. Always, it is the individual who must be addressed, located and released, underneath his misery and his hunger and his destitution. That whatever may be blocking his way to his own center where his altar may be found, this must be removed."[33] In the spirit of *ubuntu*, contemplative activism seeks to liberate both the oppressor and the oppressed.

The mystic – and the contemplative activist congregation - realizes that the rich and the poor, the oppressor and the op-

31 Howard Thurman, "Mysticism and Social Action: Lawrence Lectures and Discussions with Dr. Howard Thurman *(London: International Association for Religious Freedom, 2014), Kindle Location, Kindle Location, 177-179.*

32 Ibid., Kindle location, 235-236.

33 Ibid., Kindle location, 249-251. Ibid.

pressed, may be equally alienated from their deepest selves, despite their economic and social differences. The soul-destroying nature of poverty and injustice is obvious and must be addressed both politically and personally. Contrary to superficial thinking, the powerful and wealthy perpetrators of injustice are also in spiritual jeopardy. They may have gained the world – mesmerizing crowds and achieving political power, receiving adulation and unquestioned loyalty from their followers or seeking power by bowing down before self-absorbed politicians – only to lose their souls. As we observe the power brokers of right-wing politics and white Christian nationalism, it is evident that bravado and boasting often hides anxiety, insecurity, and envy. It is evident in those who want to placard the Ten Commandments in every public place while choosing to circulate unsubstantiated conspiracy theories, promote incivility, and support prevaricating politicians. Purveyors of racial division often sacrifice their souls and intimate relationships for short-term political gain or a sense that, even though their lives are difficult, they are better than immigrants or persons of color. Some are willing to destroy democracy and put their own well-being at risk just to maintain their sense of superiority.

There are times persons and congregations may need to play spiritual and political hardball (protesting, picketing, lobbying, boycotting) to confront injustice, racism, sexism, homophobia, and ecological exploitation. We may have to make "good trouble", as John Lewis counsels, to face down those who would destroy the nation and the human and non-human world for power and profit. As citizens, Christians, and congregations, we may have to wield power to heal our social order. There are times in which demonstrations, boycotts, and non-violent civil disobedience are necessary to effect change. But, we must always remember the interdependence of our humanity and the humanity of those whom we challenge. We can picket and pray. In caring for the health of our own souls, we promote the spiritual health of those whose injustice we challenge. In Thurman's language, oppressors may need to be "shocked" out of their complacency, sense of entitlement, and assumptions of privilege and superiority. The goal of prophetic political challenge is to agitate the comfortable and awaken them to their deeper humanity as well as the humanity of those who are harmed by their actions or apathy. In Thurman's words:

> What is important for the mystic is that the purpose of the shock treatment is to hold before the offender a mirror that registers an image of himself, that reflects the image of those who suffer at his hands. The total function of such action is to tear men from any alignments that prevent them from putting themselves in the other person's place, but it must never be forgotten that the central concern of the mystic is to seek to remove anything that prevents the individual from free and easy access to his own altar-stair that is in his own heart.[34]

In being shocked out of complacency and privilege and sometimes intentional injustice, the oppressor is given the opportunity to reclaim her or his own soul and discover her or his solidarity with all creation in God's beloved community. The healing of the oppressor becomes a catalyst for the embodiment of God's vision of Shalom in daily interactions and political and business decision-making. In seeking Shalom, we aim at reconciliation and unity, and have as our goal healing the divisions of politics, religion, economics, and race.[35]

Nurturing a Robust and Activist Progressive Spirit

The prophetic ministry of the church joins the journey inward and outward, contemplation and action. The movement of prophetic transformation is deepened by hours listening for God's still, small voice. Our own deep faith enables us to see the image

34 Ibid., Kindle location, 270-274.

35 For more on Thurman's vision, see Bruce Epperly, *Prophetic Healing: Howard Thurman's Vision of Contemplative Activism* (Richmond, IN: Friends United Press, 2020) and *The Work of Christmas: The Twelve Days of Christmas with Howard Thurman* (Noyes, NY: Anamchara Books, 2020).

of God in others and prevents us from political and theological polarization in which we see the demonic in those who differ from us. Beneath the MAGA hat hides a child of God. Beneath the hate spewing rhetoric of a politician whose positions we challenge is a child of God in need of both blessing and challenge.

Centering Prayer. As Christians, we can grow spiritually from the long tradition of Christian practices as well as from practices that join the wisdom of East and West. Meditative practices foster resilience, bolster patience for the long haul of social change, and join us in the spirit with those whose viewpoints we protest and challenge. As a first-year student in college, I learned Transcendental Meditation, also known as TM, a Hindu meditation technique adapted to the needs of busy Westerners. In TM, the practitioner focuses on a mantra, or Sanskrit word, which we repeat over and over, fifteen to twenty minutes twice each day. The popularity of TM led to a revival of the Christian practice of Centering Prayer. Centering Prayer involves the following steps:

» A comfortable position, sitting in a chair or cross legged.
» The repetition of a meaningful word that speaks to your spirit such as, "love," "God," "Spirit," "peace," "Je-sus." One of the prayer words I use is "God's light" with "God" on the inhale and "light" on the exhale.
» If thoughts intrude, bring your focus back to your prayer word without judgment.
» After 15-20 minutes, conclude with a prayer of gratitude and openness to God's guidance.

Christian Darshan/Seeing the Divine in Everyone. In Hinduism, *Darshan* means seeing a holy person or divinity. This practice of seeing God in one of God's representatives is similar to the Christian practice of meditating on icons, or windows to the Holy. If God is present in all creation, then everyone reveals God to us. Beneath the exterior, we can, as Mother (Saint) Teresa says, see God in all God's distressing disguises. Spoken to another person or internally, this East-West practice is similar to Hindu *na-*

maste, "the divine in me greets the divine in you," or the Christian salutation, "the Spirit in me greets the Spirit in you."

While it is simple to see the divine presence in people whom we love or who are our allies, seeing the Holy is difficult when we're talking about a white Christian nationalist, a supporter of Moms for Liberty (described by the Southern Poverty Law Center as a right-wing extremist group), or political personages routinely hated by the left, such as Donald Trump, Tucker Carlson, Lauren Boebert, or Marjorie Taylor Green. Yet, to be prophetic healers, we must look deeper than their hate-filled rhetoric and sloganeering. We can oppose their policies with all our heart, and also see divinity in them.

In this practice, whenever you are tempted to demean or hate someone of a different political perspective, see a light shining from them, an inner light of which they might not even be aware.

You may also choose to see your image of Jesus superimposed upon their face. As the objects of our hate and scorn, they are the "least of these" for us. Deep down, we are connected despite their political views and our tendency to demonize them.

Our prayers do not lessen our quest for justice but inspire us to treat our opponents with respect and look for points of common ground. Finding these points of common ground may be nearly impossible at first glance, but deep down, we both want to be happy, be loved, and live meaningful lives. Often their anger and incivility, their quest for power, is the result of unhealed childhood trauma and the need to be center stage. We can pray for the healing of their – and our – memories and trauma, even as we challenge the behaviors and policies can emerge from a diseased spirit.

Lovingkindness Meditation. In speaking of the human journey, the North African theologian Augustine of Hippo asserted that "our hearts are restless until we find our rest in God." C.S. Lewis similarly described moments in which he was "surprised by joy," the experience of God's presence, for which he had consciously or unconsciously been seeking. In Buddhism, there is a meditation or prayer in which one gazes upon the world and whispers:

> May all sentient beings be happy.

From recognizing the quest for happiness that all seek, often in ways that are spiritually or relationally harmful, the practitioner prays that we all experience the true happiness of enlightenment or relationship with God.

In this practice, adapted to Christian imagery, one might say the following:

> May all beings experience authentic joy, which comes from experiencing the Holy.
>
> May (a particular person) experience authentic joy, which comes from experiencing the Holy.
> May (members of a particular group, for example, MAGA followers, Moms for Liberty, Hamas, Israeli leaders) experience authentic joy, which comes from experiencing Christ's presence in their lives.

Fight hard for justice and peace. Protest climate denial and environmental destruction. Stand with the oppressed, recognizing that there is no "other." We are all joined in the Spirit, and true justice comes from reverence and reconciliation, not hatred and diminishment.

PRACTICING THE PEACEABLE REALM

Awe came upon everyone because many wonders and signs were being done through the apostles. All who believed were together and had all things in common; they would sell their possessions and goods and distribute the proceeds to all, as any had need. Day by day, as they spent much time together in the temple, they broke bread at home and ate their food with glad and generous hearts, praising God and having the goodwill of all the people. And day by day the Lord added to their number those who were being saved. (Acts 2:43-47)

I began the chapter on progressive Christian spirituality with words from Catholic theologian Karl Rahner, "the Christian of the future will be a mystic, or they shall not exist at all." The chapters on prophetic progressivism might bear a similar maxim, "the Christian of the future will be prophetic, or they shall not exist at all." Grounded in the Hebraic prophetic vision and Jesus' incarnational realm of healing and hospitality, the early Christian community embodied an alternative to insular and legalistic forms of Judaism and the violent and coercive political policies of Rome. A minority community, living by alternative vision of God and the world, the early Christian movement shared all things in common, brought forth one another's gifts without envy, and followed their savior in welcoming the least, lost, and lonely as full members of the realm of God. The good of one was essential to the good of all, and healthy communities support the well-being of each member.

The early Christian community made up its theology as it went along, drawing on the wisdom of their Hebraic parents, listening to stories about Jesus, and discerning the Living Christ in their midst and following the movements of the Spirit wherever She would lead them. From initially focusing its mission on the Jewish community, the followers of Jesus expanded their theology and understanding of salvation to include the whole Earth. The process took time, and we are still struggling to be global and inclusive in our theology, spirituality, ethics, and politics, but one step at a time the early Christian movement welcomed persons of all cultures and communities. There is always the temptation to focus solely on our own people and isolate ourselves from those who differ, succumbing to xenophobia, homophobia, racism, isolation, and classism. But, the way of Jesus and the prophets says "yes" to the wondrous diversity of life, and nurtures diversity as a reflection of God's kindom on earth.

Not yet bound by static doctrines, inflexible rules, and hierarchical ecclesiology, the early church, like the Spirit of which Jesus spoke, "blows where it chooses, and you hear the sound of it, but you do not know where it comes from or where it goes" (John 3:8). Only later did the church, fearing diversity and change, and focusing on authority and power rather than gospel experience, turn away from the Liberating Spirit of its youth to heresy hunting, hierarchical governances, authoritarian leadership, misogyny, patriarchy, and the unhealthy marriage of church and state. As Jesus discovered in the wilderness, there is always temptation to embrace the love of power rather than the power of love. There is always the temptation to swap the inclusiveness signaled by your "WWJD" – what would Jesus do hat – for exclusiveness of a

"MAGA" helmet and its religious equivalents and their embrace of racism, xenophobia, heresy hunting, and demagoguery.

The aim of progressive Christian political involvement is healing and repairing and reaching across divisions and diversities to realize God's Beloved Community in the struggles of family, congregation, national, and planetary living. Progressive Christianity is called to hold in creative tension activism aimed at realizing the Beloved Community in politics and economics and also affirming the importance of diverse viewpoints in religion, politics, and economies. We do not want a theocracy but a Peaceable Realm in which diversity leads to creative synthesis and the joining of maximal freedom with equally maximal community and global responsibility.

Theology Makes a Difference.

A major theme of this text is that theology and spirituality are practical and political in nature. What we believe shapes our character, values, and politics. A God whose power is loving and authority is relational is very different in impact than a God whose power is authoritarian and authority is monarchical. I observed a contrasting example of theology in practice and a dramatically different vision of God on January 6, 2024, three years to the day after domestic terrorists occupied the Capitol with murder on their minds. On my newsfeed, I received a document, reporting a Truth Social video reposted by Donald Trump, entitled "God Made Trump." Imitating Paul Harvey's "God Made a Farmer," the video began with a photo connecting God's vision for the planet with Trump's birthday, "And on June 14, 1946, God looked down on his planned paradise and said, 'I need a caretaker.' So God gave us Trump," Trump is described as a Messianic figure, anointed by God, called to destroy his opponents, "fight the Marxists" and "call out the fake news for their tongues as sharp as a serpent's." The video and Trump's embrace of it reflected the false theology that Trump alone can bring us back to primordial perfection! Employing Biblical language, mimicking the prophet Isaiah Trump is described as the one who "cares for the flock, shepherd of mankind, who will never leave or forsake them."[36]   Ironically, there is nothing about prayer, spirituality, Jesus, compassion, or forgiveness in the video even though it is clearly addressed to "evangelical" Christians.

As I pondered this video, wondering if Trump really sees himself as a Messianic figure or if this is a way of inspiring easily mesmerized and manipulated Christians eager to regain power and defeat their foes, I reflected on the vision of God revealed in the video: an authoritarian and vindictive deity with no compassion except for the chosen flock; no focus on prayer or spirituality; emphasis on economic gain and defeat of foes. In other words, a coercive, monarchical, punitive, and violent god, whose love is limited and who desires adulation and uniformity, and scorns diversity and creativity. A god who is transactional, and graceless, the master of the *quid pro quo*. A god very different from Abraham Lincoln's response to a companion regarding prayers for the Union: "My concern is not whether God is on our side; my greatest concern is to be on God's side, for God is always right." The question can be asked, "Do our biases reflect our image of God's nature? Or does our image of God's nature reflect our biases? Or, is it a combination of the two in the reality that religion can be the source of the greatest compassionate generosity and the most diabolical violence?"

Progressive Christians choose another vision of God: a relational, empathetic, graceful, and all-embracing God, who loves diversity and nurtures creativity, and who invites us to infuse our political lives with spiritual values. A God who inspires sacrifice, mercy, grace, compassion, and inclusiveness among God's follow-

---

36   Alia Shaib, ""Trump shares bizarre video declaring 'God made Trump,' suggesting he is embracing a messianic image," Business Insider, January 6, 2024. Trump Shares Bizarre Video Declaring: 'God Made Trump' (businessinsider.com) / For the video: Trump Posts Video Calling Himself a God-Given "Caretaker" and "Shepherd to Mankind" | Watch (msn. com)

ers. A loving God inspires a politics of compassion and hospitality and a politics that joins order, the rule of law, and safe boundaries, with care for all God's children, whether human or non-human. The relational God possesses authority and power and persists until Shalom is embodied in our institutions, whose values are defined by love and compassion not hatred, division, and destruction.

There is Only One World

Influenced by Augustine and Martin Luther, Christians have often spoken of the relationship of the church and government in terms of two different planes, "two kingdoms," each requiring vastly different and often contrasting values. From this perspective, in their immediate relationships and in the church, the Christian lives by the law of love, sacrificing for their neighbor and putting love above power. In their public life, in contrast, Christian wields power with wisdom and yet nevertheless can wield the sword to destroy their opponents and the infidel. In the scrum of politics, soon wisdom and compassion are abandoned to hold onto power. We can be kind to our neighbors at the micro level, from this perspective, and also support policies that separate children from their parents on the USA borderlands, drastically cut social welfare programs, and shout "drill, baby, drill," despite the realities of climate change, and still call ourselves Christians. We can claim to be pro-life, while advocating for draconian laws prohibiting abortion, and seeking to eliminate programs that provide food assistance and medical care for pregnant women, infants, and children. We can preach the prosperity gospel in our congregations, connecting wealth with faith, and live by scarcity in the body politic, cutting budgets and demonizing people on welfare, in terms of programs that make prosperity possible among the economically marginalized and vulnerable. We forget that biblically speaking a nation's prosperity is grounded in justice, care for all its citizens, welcome of immigrants, and support of global justice and planetary healing. Today's USA Christianity, especially conservative

Christianity, has placed individualism and unrestrained capitalism ahead of the communitarian and safety net economics of the New Testament. The love of power promulgated by megachurch political leaders and prevaricating politicians has eclipsed the power of love taught by Jesus. When Jesus preaches feeding the hungry, conservative politicians drown out Jesus' voice with "every person for themselves."

According to the Lord's Prayer, there is only one world and all of us are God's children. God's world in the here and now, joining heaven and earth, and compassion and politics. As followers of Jesus, we are to pray and act that God's realm will be embodied on earth as it is in heaven, and work toward this vision in every aspect of life. While we recognize the inherent coerciveness of governmental agencies in enforcing laws that promote public safety and environmental protection and the need to have effective border and immigration policies and national security, our goal in government and personal life is to follow God's way of peace and healing.

As impersonal as governments may seem to be, governments don't make decisions, people do. Accordingly, leaders and politically active citizens, and followers of Jesus must be guided by the horizons of prophetic justice and Christ-like love in foreign policy, economics, immigration, and human rights.

While institutions are not persons, institutional policies are guided by personal decisions. Morality and healing should guide our leadership and political involvement even when we need to make difficult decisions. Even when tough decisions need to be made, our decisions should be guided by the prophetic spirit of Jesus' Sermon on the Mount and Jesus' first public homily (Luke 4:18-19), the classic and oft-repeated mantra of this book, guiding the fusion of Progressive Christian theology, politics, and spirituality:

> *The Spirit of the Lord is upon me,*
> *because he has anointed me*

to bring good news to the poor.
He has sent me to proclaim release to the captives
and recovery of sight to the blind,
to set free those who are oppressed,
to proclaim the year of the Lord's favor.

Noted throughout this text as a Progressive Christian mantra, these words are both personal and political, and join individual, social, and planetary healing. Our political policies need to be guided by lovingkindness. Our goal should be further God's realm, act with compassion, and enforce laws with care and justice.

Practicing the Peaceable and Practical Realm in Politics

Christians cannot avoid being political. The questions are: How does our faith shape our politics? Will our politics heal or harm, reconcile or divide, embrace or reject? Progressive Christians are challenged to balance realism and idealism in the political realm. We aim to the far horizons of the moral and spiritual arcs of history. We visualize the Peaceable Realm, the Realm of God, taking form in our communities and congregations. We aim high, guided in the conflicts of history by the prophetic vision:

The wolf shall live with the lamb;
the leopard shall lie down with the kid;
the calf and the lion will feed together,
and a little child shall lead them.
The cow and the bear shall graze;
their young shall lie down together;
and the lion shall eat straw like the ox.
The nursing child shall play over the hole of the asp,
and the weaned child shall put its hand on the adder's den.
They will not hurt or destroy
on all my holy mountain,

for the earth will be full of the knowledge of the LORD
as the waters cover the sea. (Isaiah 11:6-9)

God aims high in the quest for Shalom and demands that same idealism from God's followers, as the biblical tradition affirms. God's presence in history is also contextual and shaped by the realities of history. God doesn't work with history, communities, nations, or persons in the abstract, rather God is present as the goad toward justice and compassion in relationship to concrete, conflictual, and imperfect situations, persons, and governments.

The relational God described by progressive theology is guided by the vision of truth, beauty, and goodness, and mediates the divine vision to imperfect and at times feuding institutions and political leaders. Prophetic politics are healing politics and also pragmatic politics that join heaven and earth, challenging injustice and also moving the moral and spiritual arcs of history forward one step at a time, looking toward the ultimate realm of Shalom and living in the realm of penultimate, often plodding movements, toward healing and wholeness. No one captures God's prophetic pragmatism and prophetic pragmatism needed for our time better than the philosopher Alfred North Whitehead.[37] The Ultimate Empath, guided by the divine vision of truth, beauty, and goodness, God is also the Ultimate Visionary, Realist, Relativist, and Pragmatist, in God's relationship to the concrete realities of our lives:

> The initial aim is the best for that impasse. But if the best be bad, then the ruthlessness of God can be personified as Ate, the goddess of mischief. The chaff is burnt. What is inexorable in God, is valuation as an aim towards 'order.'"[38]

---

37 For a number of years, I had used the term "prophetic pragmatism," before discovering the term had also been coined by philosopher Cornel West.

38 *Process and Reality,* Corrected Edition, ed. Griffin & Sherburne, New York: The Free Press, 1978, 244)

God deals with historical and political limits and so do we. God in the flesh works with fleshly situations and human obstinance as well as human compassion. This is the same for us in our congregations, communities, and national politics. Looking toward the far horizon, we take one step at a time toward realizing God's realm. This process is always too slow for the ideologue who is tempted to sacrifice the good for the perfect. The apostle Paul models progressive Christian pragmatism in his letter to the Philippians:

> Not that I have already obtained this or have already reached the goal, but I press on to lay hold of that for which Christ has laid hold of me. Brothers and sisters, I do not consider that I have laid hold of it, but one thing I have laid hold of: forgetting what lies behind and straining forward to what lies ahead, I press on toward the goal, toward the prize of the heavenly call of God in Christ Jesus. (Philippians 3:12-14)

Keep your eyes on the prize! There are times when radical change may be necessary and unjust institutions deconstructed. Our institutional leaders always move too slowly for prophetic spirits, especially in our current divided government in which many leaders, claiming to be Christian, are hellbent on destroying governmental programs for the vulnerable and poor, reducing human rights, eliminating environmental protection, and promoting division, seeing any compromise as treason to their cause. While we must be equally strong in supporting our viewpoints, we must avoid the idolatries of power, race, and privilege. In a divided government, we must be realistic in terms of what we can achieve, whether in terms of gun safety and control, reparations for slavery and genocide, and response to climate change. We must be open to change and compromise when it is necessary to achieve penultimate goods that will save lives, promote diversity and human rights, and protect the planet. Compromise is painful and we must be careful not to sacrifice our values and faith in the process. But, just as the progressive Paul and the conservative Jerusalem church leadership compromised to welcome Gentiles into the Christian movement, we must look for ways realistically and pragmatically to widen the circle of compassion, while protecting human rights and the environment.

A moment in the life of the early Christian community reflects this spirit of prophetic pragmatism. The early Christian movement aimed at economic justice in which property and wealth were shared for the common good (Acts 2:43-47, Acts 4:32-37). In their quest for Beloved Community, however, the movement omitted fully to realize its goal of economic wellbeing for all. Acts 6:1-6 describes the apostles' response to unintentional injustice.

> *Now during those days, when the disciples were increasing in number, the Hellenists complained against the Hebrews because their widows were being neglected in the daily distribution of food. And the twelve called together the whole community of the disciples and said, "It is not right that we should neglect the word of God in order to wait on tables. Therefore, brothers and sisters, select from among yourselves seven persons of good standing, full of the Spirit and of wisdom, whom we may appoint to this task, while we, for our part, will devote ourselves to prayer and to serving the word." What they said pleased the whole community, and they chose Stephen, a man full of faith and the Holy Spirit, together with Philip, Prochorus, Nicanor, Timon, Parmenas, and Nicolaus, a proselyte of Antioch. They had these men stand before the apostles, who prayed and laid their hands on them.*

Without defensiveness, the Jerusalem leadership recognized its unintentional omissions, the harm done to Gentile Christians, and then rectified the situation by expanding the organizational structure of the early church to be more effective in its mission. In that spirit, we need to be open to let go of past structures, now dysfunctional and unjust, and seek to expand the circles of justice, equity, reverence for life, and environmental protection in the concrete situations of our lives. We need to recognize the ambiguity built into our citizenship and privilege: we will always be complicit in relationship to some forms of coercion and injustice.

Our perspectives are limited by age, gender, sexual identity, and social location, and it is easy to overlook the experiences of historically marginalized people.

Order as well as novelty depend on adequate law enforcement and national security. We need to secure borders as well as city streets and that requires law enforcement and the threat of incarceration. The justice system may need to punish as well as reform those whose behavior harms individuals and the common good. Even here, we must be motivated by the vision of the "more perfect union" of "liberty and justice for all" in our political lives and compassion and healing in our congregational lives. We must challenge our own perspectives – and seek to be more faithful to God's vision - as we seek to understand the experience of others and shape the contours of our nation's future.

We cannot neglect our prophetic ministry even when we must seek penultimate solutions. We must not jettison prophetic protest and idealism, even as we compromise to secure the most effective ways to end poverty, secure justice, protect the nation, respond to climate change, and widen our circle of concern from self-interest and national wellbeing to world loyalty.

Nurturing a Robust and Activist Progressive Spirit

We should never settle for mediocrity or betray our principles in the quest to join the idealism of prophetic ministry with the realism of pragmatic achievement. The interplay of idealism and realism, similar to the synthesis of innovation and tradition, are necessary for moving forward the moral and spiritual arcs of history. As I've noted several times in this text, we should expect great things from God and great things from ourselves in politics as well as personal relationships. Still, the movements of the moral and spiritual arcs of history often move slowly, pushed forward by acts of justice and reconciliation, delayed by hopelessness, cynicism, incivility, and injustice. We may need to aim at joining proximate achievements and final goals as we seek to be God's companions in healing the soul of our nation and the planet. There are times God must deal with the "best for that impasse" in the movement toward Shalom, and there are times we must do likewise, recognizing that small gains are preferable to failure, and the great change often is a matter of steps forward, one after another, until we reach our goals. As I ponder the often ponderous movements of politics and the role of faith in shaping history, I am reminded of John Henry Cardinal Newman's poem, "Pillar of the Cloud":

> Lead, Kindly Light, amid the encircling gloom,
> Lead Thou me on!
>   The night is dark, and I am far from home—
> Lead Thou me on!
>   Keep Thou my feet; I do not ask to see
>   The distant scene,—one step enough for me.[39]

Spirituality is about one step at a time moving ourselves and our world forward, falling and getting back up, deepening our faith and healing the world, while always gazing at the far horizons of God's dream of Shalom.

One Step at a Time. In this meditative prayer, we once again ponder first steps in our spiritual and faith lives. Knowing that "Rome was not built in a day," and that "for everything there is a season," begin this practice with silence, breathing deeply God's inspiration and exhaling any stress or anxiety. Then take a moment to ask for God's wisdom as you embark on a mini "vision quest," prayerfully considering the following:

» Your current spiritual challenges and insight in moving forward in addressing these challenges.

» The most pressing social and political challenges we face as a nation and planet.

» After identifying these challenges, ponder first steps you can take to respond. (The first steps can be as simple as changing your dietary habits to be healthier for yourself and the plan-

---

39 Henry Cardinal Newman, 1833

et, simplifying your life to liberate yourself from the bondage of consumerism, becoming more financially supportive of groups seeking social justice and planetary healing. On the macro level, a first step might be contacting your representatives regarding a political concern, volunteering for a candidate or initiative, or studying about a particular area of concern such as climate change, white nationalism, racism, scriptural bases for discrimination against the LGBTQ+ community and alternative understandings of scripture.)

» Praying for guidance and energy to begin these first steps as you move toward God's horizon of peace, justice, and Earth care.

This same exercise can be employed as a group vision quest to help your congregation find its spiritual and political vocation.

Common Ground. One of the greatest challenges of our time is to find common ground across political and theological differences. Even those of us who claim to be progressive Christians and holistic thinkers sometimes find ourselves caught up in binary thinking, creating boundaries of us versus them and demonizing those who differ from us. In this exercise, begin once more with prayerful quiet, asking for God's guidance in leading you in paths of reconciliation.

» Visualize a political, religious, or social "other," noting your feelings toward them.

» Then, look deeper, opening to "that of God," as the Quakers say, within them. Ask for the ability to bless and be blessed by them.

» Now, ponder someone in your circle of friends or acquaintances who falls into the category of "other." Visualize the divine within them.

» Pray to discern an area where you can find common ground either in belief, intention, or action. (Sharing care for children in your community, reaching out to single mothers, volunteering at a soup kitchen, working on a disaster relief project.)

» If you are able to find common ground, then you may choose to move from hands-on support to public policy common ground. (For example, promoting community programs that provide assistance to houseless people, single pregnant mothers, playgrounds for children.)

» Pray for other ways you can work together to bring God's realm to the community in which you live.

» You might choose to pray together with persons of different faiths and political beliefs, including fellow Christians, and in these prayers, letting go of your need for your companion to pray as you do, but seeing the quest for spiritual growth in their more hierarchical or masculine language.

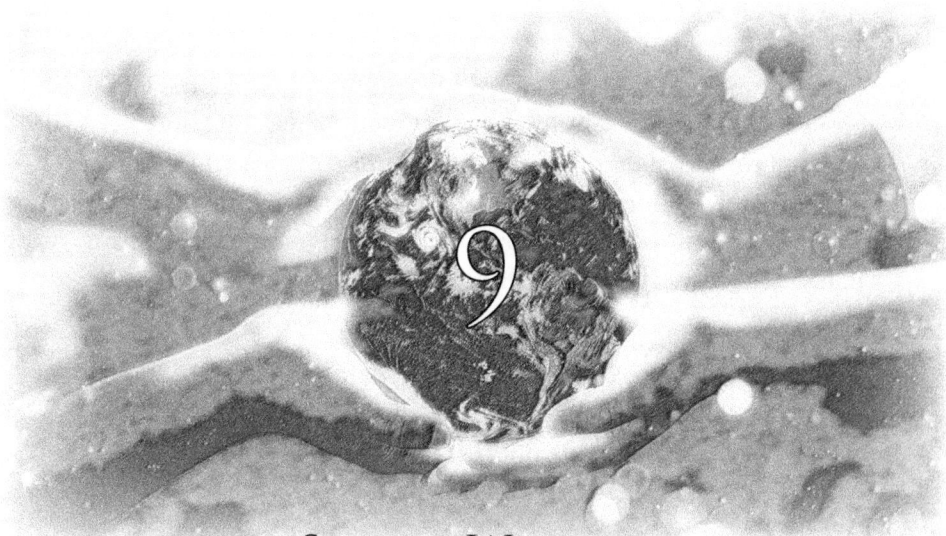

Saving Witness

I don't know Who – or what – put the question. I don't know when it was put. I don't even remember answering. But at some moment I did answer Yes to Someone – or something – and from that hour I was certain that existence is meaningful and, that, therefore, my life, in self-surrender, had a goal. From that moment I have known what it means "not to look back" and "to take no thought for the morrow."[40]

From one ancestor he made all peoples to inhabit the whole earth, and he allotted the times of their existence and the boundaries of the places where they would live, so that they would search for God and perhaps fumble about for him and find him—though indeed he is not far from each one of us. For "In him we live and move and have our being"; as even some of your own poets have said, "For we, too, are his offspring." (Acts 17:26-28)

Growing up in the Baptist church, we were told it was our obligation to tell the stories of Jesus. Souls were at stake, not only in far off Africa and India, but right in our home town. We heard

---

40   Dag Hammarsjold, *Markings* (New York: Knopf, 1964), 205.

stories of missionaries who risked life and limb to share the Good
News that Jesus Saves. Without that Good News, lost souls were
doomed to eternal damnation. I recall summer revival meetings in
our hometown church, and "came forward," the Baptist terms for
"accepting Jesus as your personal savior," at age nine, at Leonard
Eilers' revival meeting, "The Roundup for God." I was raised on
songs like:

> Rescue the perishing, care for the dying,
> Snatch them in pity from sin and the grave;
> Weep o'er the erring one, lift up the fallen,
> Tell them of Jesus, the mighty to save.[41]

Our mission was global, to reach the places of darkness across
the globe and to have "crusades" for soul winning and salvation
giving.

> We've a story to tell to the nations,
> that shall turn their hearts to the right,
> a story of truth and mercy,
> a story of peace and light,
> a story of peace and light.
> For the darkness shall turn to dawning,
> and the dawning to noonday bright;
> and Christ's great kingdom shall come on earth,
> the kingdom of love and light.[42]

We felt the burden of salvation and could make the difference
between life and death now and for eternity by our witness. We
progressive Christians are not big on witness. Few of us would dare
to witness to someone else about the superiority of our church's
beliefs or assume that their salvation depends on reciting a creed
or attending our church. We might share an event at our church
or dare to invite someone to a service, but we would feel uncom-
fortable attempting to lead someone to Christ. We have rightly

41   "Rescue the perishing," Fanny J. Crosby
42   "We've a Story to Tell to the Nations," H. Ernest Nichol

abandoned unilateral missions, evangelistic colonialism, and the denigration of indigenous peoples and the great wisdom traditions. We have rightly replaced "what man's burden" with "the burden of interdependence." We have rightly affirmed that God's love embraces everyone, God's revelation is universal, and salvation is offered to all, regardless of religion and culture. Jesus saves, and so does Buddha (although some say Buddha recycles!), following the Tao, chanting "Hare Krisha," praying at a First American sweat lodge, or claiming the wisdom of our Good Ancestors as African Yoruba/Ifa practices. We have rightly affirmed that we can be inter-spiritual or hybrid Christians, committed to the way of Jesus, and open to learning from other religious traditions. We see the rise of pluralism as an opportunity for spiritual growth and democratic flourishing and not a threat to our way of life or religion. We feel comfortable with mosque, ashram, synagogue, and sweat lodge. Yet, the future of our nation and planet may hinge on a vital progressive Christian movement joining faith, democracy, pluralism, and earth care in honest and humble ways.

I am still an evangelical Christian at heart, although I am also theologically a progressive and global Christian. I left the Baptists of my youth, first in spirit and then in body, only two years after my conversion, due to a family trauma that occurred when my father was fired from his small-town Baptist pulpit. Before I heard the word, "deconstruction," I was spiritually "deconstructed." I found my way back to a progressive Christian faith through Transcendentalism, Buddhism and Hinduism, and psychedelics. In October 1970, I found the Holy once more in a gentle and unobtrusive way, similar to Dag Hammarskjold - in fact, I had never been lost, for God was with me – when I learned Transcendental Meditation as a first-year college student and returned to a progressive American Baptist Church, adjacent to my college. From then on, and perhaps all my life, I have said "yes" and have not looked back as I seek to be open to the Millisecond Coming of Jesus, God's moment by moment inspiration, God's reality in whom "I live and move and have my being."

This book is a testimony to our times. As progressive Christians, we are not worried about the destiny of peoples' eternal souls apart from an encounter with Christ. We are struggling to find a way forward to save people in this lifetime, challenge our evangelical kin to reclaim the gospel Jesus, to rescue the soul of our nation, to heal our planet and save it from those who willfully and purposefully destroying it from profit, privilege, and power, and bring about God's realm "on earth as it is in heaven." We have a burden, but it transcends race, gender, culture, sexual identity, religion, and nation of origin. Our burden is to share good news of an alternative vision of our nation and the planet, one of unity, peace, creativity, healing, diversity, cooperation, and Earth care. The stakes are high! The survival of democracy and the survival of the planet are in the balance. The lives of asylum seekers and victims of climate related famine and war are in the balance.

We are often embarrassed to call ourselves "Christian." With Brian McLaren, we ask, "Do I Stay Christian?" when the worst perpetrators of destruction, demagoguery, and division are our fellow Christians and the Orange Jesus to whom they pledge allegiance and whose mission of scorched earth politics has eclipsed the message of Jesus, the prophets, and the alternative vision of the Sermon on the Mount in the strategies of many conservative Christians.

Hope is in short supply these days as we look at climate change and our own precarious democracy. Yet, we have a mission of our own as progressive Christians: To be God's companions in healing the world and our nation, and we can't do it alone. We've a story to tell the nation and seek to tell it in welcoming and affirming ways, in ways that honor choice, respect diversity, and recognize that God's revelation is broadcast generously. We aren't giving people what they don't have or rescuing them from a God for whom hell is the destiny for unbelievers. Yet, we are sharing a story of healing and community in desperate times when our message may be a tipping point in national and planetary healing.

Hope That Transforms Us and the World

There are grounds for hope. A recent Pew Research study, "Spirituality Among Americans," notes the following:

> 7 in 10 U.S. adults describe themselves as spiritual in some way. Nearly half say they are both religious and spiritual, which is to say they participate in religious institutions as well as have personal spiritual practices or ways of thinking about the world that aren't necessarily based on a formal religious tradition. 22% of U.S. adults say they are "spiritual but not religious." 21% say they are neither spiritual nor religious. And 10% say they are religious but not spiritual.[43]

While we recognize and affirm the positive values of our changing religious landscape, it is clear that the majority of our American kin, whether MAGA hatted or agnostic, are in quest of a connection with a reality greater than themselves. This is good news, for openness to connection with Reality is a portal to creative transformation. Conversion, a changed spirit and heart, is possible for everyone. While many persons of faith in all traditions are simply looking for an authority figure to tell them what to do, promise a positive future, and differentiate them from the infidel, I believe that openness to the Holy, to a "connection to something bigger than myself," awakens the possibility of detecting the false saviors in our midst, transcending white nationalism, and religious exclusivism, to embrace a religion of healing and wholeness, critical of "isms," and faithful to the Earth. It also awakens us to the limitations of our own viewpoints and our own need for healing and transformation.

Our witness is not for the sake of progressive Christianity, but for the emergence of a community of seekers, open to an open-spirited God, committed to growing in wisdom and stature, and faithful to the well-being of our human and non-human kin in all our diversity. Our goal is not to save the eternally lost or promote uniformity of belief, but to join the wellbeing of

43   7 in 10 U.S. adults consider themselves spiritual : NPR

our companions with the wellbeing of our nation and the planet. While our souls are in God's hands, our nation needs to be rescued from earth-destroying consumerism, injustice, and authoritarian politics. The world is saved one act at a time and our acts of hospitality and sharing may be a tipping point between survival and destruction for our democracy and the human race and its non-human companions. Perhaps, the next great mission field will be responding to conservative and evangelical Christians who can no longer abide with the small-minded vindictive God and the unholy alliance of Christianity white nationalism and unrestrained capitalism and helping those still within evangelical churches to envision a larger vision of God, Jesus, and salvation. We need to provide a clear and life-changing alternative to the idolatries of Trump Church, apocalyptic prognostication, white nationalism, divine vengeance, and toxic theology.

The Message We Share

When I was a child growing up in the Baptist church, the message of salvation was clear: if you accept Jesus as your personal savior, your sins will be forgiven, and your soul bound for heaven. Those who didn't know Christ as savior will be judged and destined for eternal damnation. "Turn or burn." We were taught that Jesus is the only way to salvation. No one comes to God but through explicit submission to Jesus through some form of the sinner's prayer. In evangelical circles, the sinner's prayer was seen as a gateway to salvation. One group, Campus Crusade for Christ, describes the sinner's prayer with these words:

> Dear Lord Jesus, I know I am a sinner. I believe You died for my sins. Right now, I turn from my sins and open the door of my heart and life. I confess You as my personal Lord and Savior. Thank You for saving me. Amen.

While I don't remember the exact words I spoke when I was saved at a small-town revival meeting in 1961, the message I accepted was clear: we are lost without God, now and in eternity, and coming to Jesus, who paid the debt incurred by sin to God by dying for ours sins, thus securing our salvation and eternal life in heaven. Each moment was a moment of decision and our souls hang in the balance. We were told that we needed to get right with God just in case we had a car accident on the way home!

Over sixty years ago, I accepted Jesus as my personal savior and I know that "through many dangers and toils and snares I have already come. 'Twas grace has hath me safe thus far and grace will lead me – and I believe everyone – home. I still accept Jesus as my savior but my Jesus is much bigger than the small-town Jesus of my childhood. I know that the Universal Christ has been my companion every step of the way and that Jesus companions every quest for truth and every seeker's steps.

I must confess that I have never heard the sinner's prayer in a progressive church, and perhaps for good reason. Most of us are universalists, who emphasize God's love over God's judgment. We are scandalized by a God who requires the death of "his" son to save humanity, and we recognize other paths to spiritual growth beyond Christianity. Eternal life doesn't play a significant role in our theology, and many theologians as well as laypersons have abandoned the evangelical vision of eternal life as morally reprehensible in its transactional nature – you must submit to God or you will be damned – as well as the notion of infinite suffering for finite sins.

The notion that no one would come to God apart from the fear of damnation found in much evangelical theology is spiritually immature and revelatory of a God less moral than a loving human parent. Scandalized by the threatening and binary vision of conversion of our evangelical and conservative Christians, we progressive Christians have too easily abandoned the idea that unique moments of religious decision can change our lives and focus on a continuity of spiritual growth from infant baptism to confirmation to adulthood. Yet, there are times in our lives when we are faced with a decision that will change everything: issues of substance use addiction, trauma, marriage, divorce, and today the survival of our nation and planet. There are times when we need to clearly say "yes" to God's vision and claim the way of Jesus as the heart of our lives. There are times when, recognizing our own inability to find healing on our own, we need to place our lives entirely in God's hands and let God take the lead in our healing process. Perhaps, we are at a such a time in our nation's history: we need grace as well as grit and the wisdom of a Higher Love to heal our nation. Nations as well as persons need to fall down on their knees, like Nineveh, and repent their sinfulness and vow to turn from life to death for their nation and the planet.

We need conversion of heart and we need revival personally, spiritually, and politically to be agents of healing for ourselves, our churches, our nation, and the planet. We need to choose life, not out of fear of God's vengeance but to ensure the wellbeing of our democracy and the planet and the flourishing of all God's children. Choosing life for the macro is connected with individual decisions in the micro and often moments of commitment in which we say "yes" to God's vision, turn from alienation and destruction, and embrace the prophetic imagination of alternative community, lifestyle, society, and planet. While we may not choose to invoke the evangelical prayers of revival preachers and parachurch groups, we may awaken to variations of the Jesus' prayer as we seek to turn around our lives and nation, not out of fear of damnation, but loyalty to God's vision of Wholeness and Shalom. I have used these prayers, and I anticipate future moments of repentance in which I call upon a wisdom, love, creativity, and power greater than my own for healing and wholeness.

> Jesus, have mercy on me, a sinner! Help me to choose love
> in my relationships and civic life!
> God heal my spirit and give me a new heart!
> God have mercy! Help me to begin again, take your path
> of wholeness and live out your
> vision of Shalom.

God save and enlighten me!
God give me a new and loving spirit!
God open my senses to the pain of the world!
God give me compassionate power to be your companion
in healing the nation and planet!
Loving God, deliver me from my addictions, and create in
me a new spirit.

We need to say "yes" as did Dag Hammarskjold. We need to repent, that is, be transformed, not out of fear or to join the salvation crowd while others burn, but to claim God's abundant life for ourselves, our families, the nation, and the world. Our healing involves personal choice, and not individualistic decision-making. We are nurtured by the Graceful Interdependence of Life and God's loving companionship and our wholeness brings wholeness to the world. Our countercultural vision of salvation shapes every aspect of our lives, including our commitment to justice, peace-making, and human and non-human rights.

Do not be conformed to this age, but be transformed by the renewing of the mind, so that you may discern what is the will of God—what is good and acceptable and perfect. (Romans 12:2)

As I noted earlier, given the reality of authoritarian, planet and democracy destroying versions of Christianity, it is vital to proclaim an affirmative life supporting vision of God. The God we believe in, and the world we perceive, shapes everything in our lives from personal economics to global ecology, to our attitudes toward strangers and persons of other religious traditions and ways of life. While there is no one set of theological doctrines that we are called to share, the principles which have guided this book invite us and others to an affirmative, justice-seeking, hospitable, and earth-affirming faith. To repeat, I believe that the witness of progressive Christian theology may be vital for giving hope and vision to evangelicals whose faith has been "deconstructed" yet still want to claim Jesus and his way as central to their lives. Briefly put and gracefully affirmed with no threat to agnostics and atheists, and our fellow conservate Christian kin, mired in individualism, nationalism, and the love of power, and the converse fear of divine judgment:

» God loves you in your uniqueness and is present in your life to heal and affirm.

» God loves everyone and embraces humankind in all its diversity.

» God "speaks" to you and to everyone.

» God's vision for you is a joyful life and a commitment to bring joy to others, personally and politically.

» God wants us to be creative and imaginative, and to exercise your agency in healing the world. You can do something beautiful for God.

» You can experience healing and transformation. By God's grace, you can change your life. You can turn around, repent, and become part of God's healthy holy adventure.

» A relationship with God, in Christ, can bring joy, confidence, and commitment to care for others.

» In relationship to God, we can do great things. We can experience and share abundant life.

» We are connected in an intricate web of relationships. What we do matters to the wellbeing of our communities and planets.

» Trusting God, we can be transformed: we can face substance use addiction, consumerism, and alienation and find peace and empowerment to become a new creation.

» The future is open and we matter to our families, communities, nation, and planet. What we do can tilt the moral and spiritual arcs toward fulfillment in our world.

» We are not alone. We have God, Jesus, and one another, and together we can do great things to heal the world.

» Nothing in life and death can separate us from the love of God, who is constantly providing us with insights and inspirations and hope for any imagined future.

» God needs us to be God's companions in healing the world. Our salvation is connected to saving the world. God's needs us to save the nation and the planet.

» What we do matters and in an "open and relational world," God needs us to embody Gods vision in our personal and political lives.

» Your life is in God's care, now and forevermore. In whatever future you face, God is with you and holds you in God's loving arms.

» Or, as I said to the children of the churches I've pastored, in shorthand: "God loves you. We love you. You matter. You can do great things with your life."

These affirmations transform lives and change the world. These affirmations are also connected to the pathways of spiritual, healing, and prophetic challenge I have described in this text. Along with our beliefs, we are given spiritual practices and ethical guidance for the pathway ahead: practices to deepen our spiritual lives, actions to promote beauty and justice in our relationships and in the world, and practical suggestions for earth care and political transformation. We are saved for the world, healed to do something beautiful for God, and loved to embrace the "other" and discover "there is no other."

How Shall We Share Our Good News?

Many progressive Christians are nervous about sharing the good news of our faith. We would feel better telling a neighbor about a book we've been reading or a film we just saw than sharing the message of Jesus. We share about the shows we stream on cable, with invitations such as "Have you seen Ted Lasso?" or the latest episode of "Midsomer Murders?" or "Are you free to join me at a Super Bowl party?" We invite friends to a concert or a bar for conversation and drinks, but seldom to church. It seems too pushy and too much like the binary Christianity that has wreaked havoc in our nation.

We aren't even sure about telling folk that we are Christians. If they are practicing Christians, we fear that they might be "evangelical" or "fundamentalist," and assume that we're intolerant, anti-science, homophobic, anti-democratic, and intolerant. As I noted earlier in this text, we worry when a friend says, "I've found Jesus." Based on past experience, we anticipate conversations about the perils of the gay agenda or the perversions of drag queens or that they will suddenly see Donald Trump as America's savior. On occasion, when I introduce myself as a Christian, I'm tempted mumble an apology in advance, "I'm not like those Christians the media highlights" or use an adjective such as "progressive" or "pro-choice" or "pro-LGBTQ+," to differentiate ourselves from the authoritarian, anti-democratic, anti-science brand of Christianity.

But, we need to claim once more the name of Jesus and the name Christian. Faith lives by what it affirms, not what it denies. In these perilous times for the nation or the planet, we need to find creative ways to share a faith without fences, absolutes, pamphlets, or spiritual laws. While we aren't the only Christians, our progressive Christian faith – and today faith needs adjectives! – needs to be proclaimed from the mountaintops to welcome searching souls and questioning companions in working to save the nation and planet and to help seekers find their way and children and youth find open-spirited responses to their questions.

There are many ways to witness. We need to "listen to our lives" to discern the right way and time to share our understanding of God's personal and planetary vision. We need to take the Quaker adage, "let your life speak" guide our witness. We must go beyond armchair Christianity to embody an open-spirited Christianity that transforms individual lives and the world as a whole. This means being committed to grow in wisdom and stature, integrity, and commitment to justice and hospitality in local and global politics. In other words, to "walk the talk." Progressive congregations need also to "let their lives speak" in the integration of solid theological reflection, spiritual practices, hospitality to strangers, community involvement, and political action for justice and peace. We have an exciting theology, spirituality, and politics and need to share our congregation's identity with joy and excitement.

Philosopher Alfred North Whitehead asserts that the higher organisms initiate novelty to match the novelties of the environment. And our national and planetary environment is definitely novel. The word "uncharted territory" has become an oxymoron, overused, and yet reflective of unanticipated changes in the environment, and the acceptance in our democracy of a prevaricating, dishonest, morally vacuous, egocentric politician as the savior of Christianity. We must acknowledge the changes and the perils of our time and be willing to not only adapt to change technologically, theologically, and spiritually, but also innovate in ways we had not previously imagined.

We must let our lives speak, and also let our companions speak. We must see them and honor them. We must listen to their lives as we share our own lives with them. Witnessing to the Living Christ is relational and not doctrinal. We must be willing to grow spiritually and intellectually in our conversations with seekers and persons of other faiths. We cannot say "Christ is the answer" without knowing the question! We are not trying to rescue the perishing or save people from hell, but welcome people to an abundant, growing, and meaningful life in which they and their children can find a framework for ethical decision making, hope for the future, and confidence to face change and tragedy.

As we let our lives speak, we need to let our theology and congregational outreach speak in novel and creative ways, true to our progressive open-ended spirit and true to embracing technologies and methodologies that address new generations on their own terms. We need to embrace new worship styles, times, and

methods even as we honor the grand hymns of faith and traditional liturgies. We need to open hands and hearts to seekers, persons
who describe themselves as spiritual but not religious, and persons
in recovery from conservative Christianity. We need to be willing
to undergo our own process of creative transformation, allowing
ourselves to be changed by our relationships with seekers and new-
comers.

As we let our lives speak, we are not called to be sophisticated
theologians or spiritual giants. Embracing and sharing some version of the affirmations of this chapter or other progressive spiritual guidance will be quite sufficient in your conversations with
seekers and troubled evangelicals. Our primary calling is making
a commitment to the integration of theological, spiritual, ethical,
and political growth, as the foundation to serve God in our relationships, congregations, and the world. The world is saved one
act at a time, and our witness can bring healing, direction, and
transformation in every encounter, when we listen to our lives and
then let our faith speak!

Nurturing a Robust and Activist Progressive Spirit

One of my favorite spiritual couplets involves the interplay
of Frederick Buechner's "listen to your life" and Parker Palmer's
"let your life speak." The journey inward and outward are one.
Contemplation leads to activism. Theological reflection inspires
changed lives. Social concern and political involvement aim at
bringing joy and possibility to our companions and prophetic
spiritual healing to our communities. In these exercises, we ground
our witness in personal relationships and the public square with
deep, whole-person spiritual and theological practices.

What Shall I Share? Many progressives are reticent about faith
sharing. We also are uncertain of how to articulate our own theology. Despite our progressive vision, we have often defined ourselves in terms of what we don't believe, and not our theological
and spiritual affirmations. Since faith lives by affirmation, by our

great "yes," we need to expand theological education and spiritual formation in congregational faith formation and preaching. Our "yes" may need to be followed by a "no" in response to injustice, xenophobia, homophobia, and theocracy, but first we must have a theological upon which to build our ethics and social concern.

In this exercise, set aside a discreet period of time, perhaps as much as thirty minutes, each day over the next week to join prayer and theological reflection. After a time of quiet prayer, begin to journal in response to the question, "What are my theological essentials?" Let these emerge and refine them over a week's period, remembering to be flexible and open to change. As you continue to reflect on your theology, ponder how you might respond to questions such as:

» What does your church believe and do your congregation's beliefs shape its practices, socially, politically, and locally in terms of service?
» What would you share with a friend or neighbor about your spiritual journey?
» How does your belief shape your social concern and political involvement?

Make a commitment to support or initiate a robust faith formation program at your church, and participate in classes, joining theological reflection and spiritual practices.

Joining the Inner and the Outer. As a college student, I encountered June O'Conner's book, inspired by her involvement in Washington D.C.'s Church of the Savior, in which she connected the "journey inward" with the "journey outward." In this interplay of solitude and activism, we can join prayer and protest and contemplating and campaigning.[44]

In this practice, daily take time for silent meditation, opening yourself to God's still, small voice. Invite God into your heart and mind, with the question, "What is my vocation in today's politics

---

44   June O'Connor, *Journey Inward, Journey Outward* (New York: Harper Collins, 1975).

and social concern?" Listen for what emerges and commit yourself to be Gods' companion in healing the world.

Blessing the Other. A spiritual affirmation I use, based on a phrase from Maxie Dunnam's *Workbook of Living Prayer,* is "I give Christ to and receive Christ from everyone I meet" or "I bless and receive a blessing from everyone I meet." Throughout the day, look deeply at those persons you encounter, saying to yourself, "I bless you in the spirit of Jesus." Let this blessing be your companion as you face a variety of situations each day. Be willing throughout the day also to be attentive to the blessings you receive from others, giving thanks for their presence in your life. There is something of God in everyone and by opening to God's presence in their lives, I may help facilitate their own spiritual growth and healing.

PROPHETIC HOPE

In hope that sends a shining ray
Far down the future's broadening way
In peace that only Thou canst give
With Thee, O Savior [Master], let me live.[45]

Look well to the growing edge!
All around us worlds are dying
and new worlds are being born;
All around us life is dying and life is being born.
The fruit ripens on the tree;
the roots are silently at work in the darkness of the earth
against a time when there shall be new leaves,
fresh blossoms, green fruit.

Such is the growing edge!
It is the extra breath from the exhausted lung,
the one more thing to try when all else has failed,
the upward reach of life when weariness closes
in upon all endeavor.
This is the basis of hope in moments of despair,
the incentive to carry on when times are out of joint
and men have lost their reason, the source of confidence

45 "O Master, Let Me Walk with Thee," George Washington Gladden

when worlds crash and dreams whiten into ash.
The birth of the child — life's most dramatic answer to
death — this is the growing edge incarnate.
Look well to the growing edge![46]

This text is a testament to hope in a time when we are tempted to give up on our nation and the planet. As I penned this book,
I was reminded of two lines from Harry Emerson Fosdick's "God
of Grace and God of Glory": "Save us from weak resignation from
the evils we deplore/Let the gift of your salvation be our glory
evermore." Without hope, the future is lost. Without hope, our
nation and planet will collapse. Without hope, our congregations
will perish and our communities implode. Yet, hope is difficult to
come by these days. A major USA political party denies climate
change, fosters election denial, jeopardizes democracy, supports
authoritarian governments, delights in ostracizing immigrants
and marginalized people, flirts with fascism and Nazism, and promotes disinformation and conspiracy theories. Its policies seem to
privilege destruction over creation, division over unity, and igno-
rance over science. A major movement in Christianity has chosen
to put its faith in culture wars and culture warriors and has denied
the hospitable and healing Christ. In contrast to earth destroying
politics and theology, strides toward climate change are made by
progressive political leaders, despite challenges from Congress and
corporations, and yet the fate of the earth as well as the future of
democracy are still in doubt. Given the membership losses and
aging demographics of our churches, not to mention the decline
of Christianity especially among young adults and youth in North
America, we wonder if there is a future for progressive Christianity. While building on the shifting sands of falsehood, ideology,
and incivility, conservative political policy, including climate and
science denial, white privilege, and incivility, conservative politics
has mesmerized a significant minority of USA citizens, and the
majority of our conservative Christian kin. Among many of our

46   Howard Thurman, *The Growing Edge*

Christian siblings allegiance to Donald Trump has supplanted the way of Jesus, whose message is seen as impractical compared to the scorched earth politics of the right. Can we hope that our conservative Christian kin will find their way back to Jesus? Can we find ways to share a hope built on the solid rock of God's love rather than the shifting sands of hatred and retribution? Can we provide guidance and hospitality to those who are struggling to reclaim the way of Jesus? Can we give your conservative Christian kin hope beyond white nationalism, individualism, free market capitalism, and transactional salvation? Can we give them hope in the love of God and the healing power of Jesus, that calls us all home?

We ask ourselves, hoping against hope: Is there a balm in Gilead? Can these dry bones live? Can our nation and planet survive the malign influence of a Christianity coopted by nationalism, climate denial, racism, and the love of power?

Hopelessness in history takes many forms. We may simply drop out, believing politics to be morally bankrupt and unredeemable, and believing that nothing we do will make a difference. In our idealism, we may choose to scorn the realities of political compromise, considering anything less than the Peaceable Kingdom, or Kindom, unworthy of our support, forgetting the wisdom of Alfred North Whitehead who states that God must even seek the best for the impasse and though the best may appear be bad, it is a better option than the alternatives. One small step forward is preferable to backward movement in the moral and spiritual arcs of history. Keeping our eyes on the prize, the vision of Shalom, we embrace a spirituality and politics of imperfection, knowing that the horizon of God's love never ceases to lure us forward. As a childhood song proclaims,

> We are climbing Jacob's ladder
> We are climbing Jacob's ladder,
> Bearers of the cross.

Every round goes higher, higher,
Every round goes higher, higher,
Bearer of the cross.

We can also sing we are "dancing Sarah's Circle, sisters, brothers all," as "on and on, the circle's moving"

Hope in a Time of Crisis

While I cannot claim to articulate the meaning of hope in its fullness, my understanding of hope involves a constellation of images, all of which are grounded in our concrete world and point us toward the future. With Howard Thurman, I see hope in the struggles of a baby bird to fly, in resilience to reach for the skies despite the limits others place upon us personally or politically, the birth of a child, and the Spring growth of flowers. I see hope in rebirth after deconstruction and in new shoots springing up after a forest fire, promising mighty trees in the future. I see hope as the growing edge that joins the far horizon of possibility – the vision of Shalom – with the conflicts and limitations of the present moment. Hope emerges when we discover that within the limits we face are also the womb of possibility.

Hope is the Sankofa bird, the Southern African image, of a bird moving forward while looking backward, building a future from the tragic past, and then looking toward the open future to inspire creative and liberating action in the future. Hope is the Pheonix rising from the ashes to soar upward, freed from the death grip of past injustice. Hope is the resurrection revealing the power of Life and Love to overcome the most desperate situations. Hope is the majestic vision of prophets such as Isaiah, who see destruction all around, and also the movements of the moral and spiritual arcs making a way in the wilderness, restoring life to the desert, and energizing those who have felt the trauma of defeat and persecution:

Have you not known? Have you not heard?
The LORD is the everlasting God,
 the Creator of the ends of the earth.
He does not faint or grow weary;
 his understanding is unsearchable. He gives power to the
faint
 and strengthens the powerless.
Even youths will faint and be weary,
 and the young will fall exhausted,
but those who wait for the LORD shall renew their strength;
 they shall mount up with wings like eagles;
they shall run and not be weary;
they shall walk and not faint. (Isaiah 40:28-31)

Hope joins imagination and concreteness, effort and grace, vision and realism, faith and doubt, the far horizon and the present moment, the cure and the disease, resilience and weariness. Inspiring agency, hope awakens to the mystery of divine providence that frees the slaves, heals the broken, and gives sight to the blind.

Backsliding is always possible. Hopeless passivity and divisive polarization are always possible. But, there is wonder and gratitude in the African American spiritual that asks, "Over and over, over and over, my soul looks back and wonders how I got over?" Hold fast to hope, God counsels. Hold fast to dreams, as Langston Hughes counsels. When dreams and hope die, then we become frozen in the present, having lost the ability to fly.[47]

Hope is a pick and shovel virtue, as my wife Kate says, that faces pain and tragedy, knowing there is more to life than defeat and death, and knowing that the soul of the nation can be revived, but only if we look fully at the present obstacles and then look more deeply to the seeds of possibility God as planet in the detritus of doom.

---

47 Langston Hughes, "Dreams."

Frameworks for Hope.

Biblical scholar and process theologian Will Beardslee once spoke of a "house for hope," a space in which hope can be sustained, energized, and enlivened. Hope needs a home. Hope needs nurture. Hope needs robust theological visions joined with spiritual practices and a healthy community that give life and empower us to claim our role as God's companions in the quest for the healed nation and the vision of the Peaceable Realm. Hope must be concrete, not abstract or ideological, flexible and creative, grounded in the now and aiming toward the horizons of Shalom. In that context, let me share a few aspects of a flexible and growing framework for hope to motivate us to embrace wisdom, courage, and activism for the living of these perilous days for our church, nation, and planet:

» *The Interdependence of Life: We are Connected and Shape Each Other and the Future. Ubuntu,* "I am because of you. We are because of one another. There is no other." Separation is a theological, economic, and political issue, that isolates us from God and our neighbor. We are connected. The hopelessness of the poor dims the souls of the wealthy. Unrest in the Middle East or Ukraine adds to the anxiety of USA school children, regardless of their ethnicity. We are intimately connected in a web of relatedness that joins all of our destinies. In the body of Christ, not only the church but the cosmos, wellbeing in one part contributes to joy of the lives of others. Conversely, injustice leads to disease in the church, politic, and planet. Hope arises because in our connection with one another and the earth, we can shape the world in positive ways, step by step embodying God's realm of Shalom. In an interdependent world, even the smallest act can tip the nation and planet from death to life.

» *The Future is Open: What We Do Matters in Healing the Earth and Our Nation.* In an open future, what we do and who we are matters. The planetary, personal, and political stories are unfinished and incomplete. We can alter the future by transforming the present. The future is not preordained by God or our political leaders, but open to change. In fact, God wants us to become change agents by using our freedom to find common ground with others and create alternative futures to the dystopian worlds imagined by – and promoted – by political leaders and apocalyptic prognosticators. Hope is grounded in the vision of an open future and horizon of possibility.

» *Small is Beautiful: The World is Saved One Moment at a Time.* In an interdependent, open and relational universe, the world is saved one act at a time. As the Talmud says, when you save one soul, or species or habitat, it is as if you are saving the world. Small acts, done with great love, as Mother (Saint) Teresa avers, heal lives and heal the planet. Hope recognizes that the results of our actions may not immediately be visible but over the long haul, commitment to acts of loving relatedness and citizenship heal the world.

» *Miracles Happen within Naturalistic Cause and Effect Relationships that Transform Lives and the World: Within Nature There is a Moral Arc that Blesses and Magnifies Our Efforts.* Margaret Mead once asserted, "Never doubt that a small group of thoughtful committed individuals can change the world. In fact, it's the only thing that ever has." While coalitions and movements are necessary, groups gathered for prayer, protest, non-violent civil disobedience, and voluntary action to improve the quality of life of others are catalytic in nature. Jesus had but a handful of women and men in his inner circle, but they changed the world. Gautama's original following was modest and yet millions have found wholeness and spiritual liberation as a result of following his teachings. Within the natural processes of cause and effect, leaps of energy and change can emerge, creating a tipping point for creative transformation and planetary healing. The hundredth monkey transforms an entire species. A thin place in which divine energy is released to supplement our efforts. When we reach out to God, power is released, as it was with the woman with the flow of blood. When we sacrifice for a greater good, our generosity may provoke change in others and activate deeper laws of nature, as did the boy with the five loaves and two fish. We matter to the future of our nation and planet and can be midwives of the miraculous, awakening divinity in everyday life and in politics. As President Barack Obama asserted, "It depends on us, on the choices we make, particularly at certain *inflection points* in history; particularly when big changes are happening and everything seems up for grabs."

» *Aim at the Horizon and Honor Small Steps Toward Shalom.* The great spiritual leader and parent of Daoism, Lao Tzu, proclaimed that "the journey of a thousand miles begins with a single step." We must have our eyes on the prize, stay focused, expect miracles, join with companions, and also look at horizons we may never reach. The prophet's dream of justice rolling like waters begins at a soup kitchen, writing a check, protesting an injustice, or calling a political leader. The first steps may seem halting and we may wonder if they really make a difference. Legislation may not achieve all we hope for. Yet, let us not despair. Let us find common cause and achieve penultimate goals on way to realizing the Beloved Community. Political and community change are messy, and we must never lose sight of God's realm embodied on earth as it is in heaven, while we also celebrate small steps toward justice, peace, and planetary transformation. Our leaders are imperfect, our laws often too modest in vision, but we must not reject the good even as we seek "the more perfect union." Think big and celebrate small gains. Let small changes inspire great goals. Alfred North Whitehead says that God's aim is the best for that impasse and that aim may, in certain circumstances be less than optimal. Yet the achievement of the best for impasse leads to greater gains in realizing God's vision of

truth, beauty, and goodness – of healing and justice – in our
body politic and planetary future.

» *God is Our Companion: God Needs Us to Heal the Earth and
Our Nation as God's Hands and Feet.* We are not alone. God
is with us. Not as coercive dictator or retributive judge. Not
as the all-determiner who despises human initiative and creativity. But, as the fellow sufferer who understands, the great
empath who feels, and joyful intimate who celebrates. God
wants us to be creative. God encourages us to use our freedom
wisely. God needs us to be God's hands and feet, God's heart
and mind, God's protest and healing touch, in our world.
Together we can, as Jesus says, do greater things than we can
imagine healing and repairing the world.

Nurturing a Robust and Activist Progressive Spirit

Hope emerges from the marriage of concrete realities and as-
pirational dreams and the recognition that the future is open and
our actions can create the world about which we dream. Hope
is not optimism, but the hard work of living with a vision that
motivates your citizenship and political action. Hope requires
spiritual commitment as well as practical agency. The words of
Theodore Parker, popularized by Martin Luther King and Barack
Obama describe the onward movement of God's vision in history
and also the need for spiritual constancy to incarnate this vision in
the ambiguities of imperfect political processes. "I do not pretend
to understand the moral universe; the arc is a long one, my eye
reaches but little ways; I cannot calculate the curve and complete
the figure by the experience of sight; I can divine it by conscience.
And from what I see I am sure it bends toward justice."

What are Your Hopes? In this spiritual practice, begin with a
time of prayerful contemplation, with the intention of discerning the hopes that will shape your life-changing activities. Breathe
deeply, considering the deepest challenges you see in your world

and the greatest obstacles to your own fulfillment and the fulfillment of those around you. Visualize possible futures that call
you forward. What energizes you and inspires your imagination?
What kind of person are you challenged to become? What first
steps do you need to take to begin to realize your hopes? Ask God's
energy and guidance to take the first steps of a never-ending journey.

What is One Thing You Can Do to Save the World? Remembering that the world is saved one action at a time, consider persons
or situations where your gifts can provide healing, wholeness, and
growth. What is the nature of the disease or brokenness you see
in that situation? Ask for God's inspiration in responding to this
situation. Visualize yourself bringing wholeness to this person.
Ask God's guidance for taking the first steps to supporting their
healing process.

Recognizing that our vocation involves our citizenship as well
as personal relationships, repeat this spiritual practice, considering prayerfully social and political situations in need of healing.
Which situations call to you personally? Ask God's guidance for
your first steps in creatively and humbly responding to this social
and political situation.

*What is One Thing Your Congregation or Community Can Do
to Help Save the World?* Many of us are part of religious communities. Our communities, like persons, also have vocations in their
larger communities. Prayerfully open to the gifts and possibilities
of your congregation. Remembering that our vocations involve
the relationship between our gifts and the world's needs, ask for
God's guidance in supporting your congregation's ministry to heal
the world. What situations are most appropriate? What might be
your congregation's first steps in healing the world? What might
you do to support this vocation of healing?

Sent Forth with God's Blessing

Recognizing the ambiguities of our lives, the struggles to be faithful, our vocation as being God's partners in saving the world, let us conclude with Reinhold Niebuhr's prayer from the *Irony of American History.*

> *Nothing that is worth doing can be achieved in our lifetime; therefore we must be saved by hope. Nothing which is true or beautiful or good makes complete sense in any immediate context of history; therefore we must be saved by faith. Nothing we do, however virtuous, can be accomplished alone; therefore we must be saved by love. No virtuous act is quite as virtuous from the standpoint of our friend or foe as it is from our standpoint. Therefore we must be saved by the final form of love which is forgiveness.*

Let us seek to follow the path of Jesus, faithful to the tasks that lie ahead of us, knowing that we are not alone and that God is with us, energizing, enlivening, enlightening, and empowering us to do small things with great love and great things with compassion and purpose. Let us claim humbly our place in healing the soul of our nation and healing the soul of Christianity. Let our light shine – God's light shine – to heal the world.

www.ingramcontent.com/pod-product-compliance
Lightning Source LLC
Chambersburg PA
CBHW031959080426
42735CB00007B/442